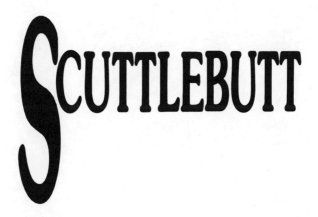

Scuttlebutt

A
Novel
by
Jana
Williams

Firebrand
Books

Writing and publishing a first novel is a highly complex process, which seems to involve equal parts of self-determination and community support. I've worked hard, but so have many people to help keep me on track. I'd like to thank them for their time and caring: Nancy K. Bereano (Firebrand Books), Margo Dunn (Ariel Books), Barbara Kuhne (Press Gang Publishers), Richard Marchand, Colin Thomas, Donna and Carol. A special thanks to C.D.

Book design by Betsy Bayley
Cover design by Betsy Bayley and Alice Muhlback
Typesetting by Bets Ltd.

Printed in the United States on acid-free paper by McNaughton & Gunn

Library of Congress Cataloging-in-Publication Data

Williams, Jana, 1950–
    Scuttlebutt : a novel / by Jana Williams.
        p. cm.
        ISBN 0-932379-89-3 (alk. paper). — ISBN 0-932379-88-5 (pbk. : alk. paper)
        I. Title.
    PS3573.I449323S35   1990
    813'.54—dc20
                                                      90-3775
                                                      CIP

Although this is a fictionalized version of my own passage through the navy's bootcamp for women—one character is very real. I'd like to dedicate this book to seaman recruit Jones. We can never be sure what our every day acts of bravery will inspire.

★ ★ ★

And to my mother. I could say the same of her.

Scuttlebutt is military slang for gossip or news.

Part One:
☆ ☆ ☆
BABY BOOTS

1

★ ☆ ☆

Roberta Weston had kissed her mother good-bye in the small Phoenix airport, hugged her hurriedly, and left the concourse nearly airborne with enthusiasm. The sun seemed particularly bright, the sky uncommonly blue. She chose to view these as omens, heralds of good fortune for launching her new life in this, her twentieth year.

But now, all remnants of her early morning enthusiasm were gone. Weston dropped her suitcase in the dimly lit hallway of the women recruits' barracks. She slumped onto the ready-made bench, sighed, and propped her elbows on her knees. Her decision to join the navy would have appealed to her father's sense of adventure. But he was dead, long dead. She cupped her chin in her hands and slowly massaged her temples. The pulse beneath her fingers stubbornly refused to be subdued. Years before his death he had quit his dreaming and started drinking. Weston removed her wire-rimmed glasses and rubbed bloodshot eyes. They burned from the cigarette smoke and forced air in planes and busses and waiting rooms. Her stomach continued to roll from the motion of a day of nonstop travel.

She slowly replaced her glasses and ran her fingers through her short brown hair. In the gloomy hallway behind her, she could hear the murmurs and whispers of the other new recruits who had trailed her from airport to airport, then finally on the interminable bus trip to Bainbridge. They all chafed at the unknown delay at the end of the journey. Weston pivoted to face them, murder on her mind. The women before her drooped in every way imaginable. If they look this bad, she thought to herself, it's not likely that I look any better. Shoulders, faces, and eyes all silently protested the physical and emotional demands pressed upon them throughout the day, and now late into the night.

Weston rose slowly from her suitcase and sighed. She made herding motions with her hands as she silently approached the group. Her voice was subdued and businesslike. "I've been asked to collect everyone's orders. Please pass them forward, quietly. Let's not forget that others are sleeping in this barracks. Let's try to keep our voices down. Or better yet, don't talk at all." When the women had formed a tight circle around her, she continued. "The watch stander has gone to wake the officer on duty. Once she arrives and checks us in, we'll be assigned a place to sleep." The faces around her brightened considerably in response.

As a child, Weston could fall asleep anywhere. One dark night, having run out of gas, she and her father began hitchhiking to the nearest town. She slept soundly as he carried her draped over one shoulder. Another time while her parents were picking cotton, she lay down at the end of the dusty row and curled herself into a ball at the base of the plants. Oblivious to the Arizona summer, she fell asleep in the open field in the welcome shade provided by the cotton. The other field workers all carefully stepped around her until one finally roused her for dinner.

Her father thought it quite an accomplishment that she was able to sleep standing up, lying down, or propped against the walls in the corner of a bus station. He used to boast loudly to his friends that she was a "natural for the rails." She had lived then for the day when he would keep his promise to her that they would become 'boes and ride the rails across the country.

Slowly, Weston brought herself back to the present. Everything ached from a day of sitting, but she was too tired to stand. She felt immeasurable relief at having arrived at bootcamp. It meant the end to the tension of traveling with a pack of puppies at her heels. It meant, she hoped, an opportunity to sleep.

★　★　★

"Momma, look at me. Can't you see I'm scared? I don't want to do this anymore. Say don't go, Momma. Say don't go."

The morning was dark, cold, strange. Weston lay immobile on her bunk, mouthing the words in her dream. Tears that had been unshed at her leave-taking gathered now under the tightly closed lids of her brown eyes. They collected like dew on her lashes. She lay coiled and rigid under the rough wool blanket.

The vision of her mother wavered as she relived again and again their final good-bye. In a slow dissolve, the scene changed to the interior of the airplane. Weston could only watch as the flight attendants swung the boarding door closed and then locked it. She was acutely aware of the Arizona sunshine that seemed to seep through every molecule of the cabin's casing. It continued illuminating her dream with a light that grew brighter and brighter until it burned her eyes.

★　★　★

"REVEILLE," an unworldly voice bellowed. A police whistle shattered the remains of her dream. Weston's eyes ripped open and then immediately closed in pain. Suspended directly over her bunk was a large florescent light that had suddenly blared to life.

"HIT THE DECK, ladies," the disembodied voice shrilled. The police whistle shrieked again.

Instinct hurled Weston from the top bunk and made her find her feet. Once she was on the floor and erect, her brain stalled in attempting to process the mayhem around her. Bedsprings groaned, locker doors slammed, and women pushed roughly by her as she clung to the metal bed frame. The initial rush of adrenalin that had fueled her leap had now turned her legs to rubber. She was still panting slightly from the harsh awakening when she felt someone grab her arm and shove her forward past the bunks.

"Put your toes on that red line and face the hallway," the woman's voice hissed. "*Hurry*. There's never much time," she added, as she pushed Weston into place. Weston felt the woman fall into place next to her. "All you have to do is stand up straight until roll call is finished," the voice continued. There was a moment's silence, and Weston could hear the echo of heels—click, click, click—striking the floor at the far end of the hallway. "And whatever you do, don't look at them. You're never supposed to actually see the officer on duty." The woman punctuated her words with a jab to Weston's ribs.

Weston determined to follow all this advice to the letter. Without her glasses, the figures lining both sides of the hallway were indistinct. She glanced down at her feet and was barely able to see the ten cold toes that covered the red line on which she stood. She turned her head imperceptibly and struggled to focus on the woman who stood next to her. The voice she had heard belonged to a tall, thin woman who was dressed in what appeared to be her grandfather's bathrobe. The woman's dark hair was pulled into a messy ponytail that hung rakishly down one side of her neck. Any comic aspect to her appearance was completely overshadowed by the determined expression on her face. The woman steadfastly ignored Weston's attention.

The drone of morning roll call seemed to Weston to be permanently mired at the far end of the barracks. She became aware of the cold from the floor creeping up the back of her calves. Her legs began to ache. For relief, she tried balancing her weight on the outer edges of her bare feet. She swayed rhythmically back and forth, squinting at her toes as they appeared and disappeared beneath the hem of her nighty.

"WESTON, R. D.," a voice roared directly in front of Weston. Her head jerked up from scrutinizing the floor and she blurted,

"Huh?" without thinking. Even before it fully crystallized on the morning air, Weston lamented its escape.

Roll call lurched to an immediate halt. Weston watched in horror as the officer on duty turned abruptly on her heel and met her face to face. Tension radiated from the two recruits flanking Weston on either side. She didn't need her glasses to easily identify the large, chromium whistle that glittered like a rare jewel against the woman's starched white shirt.

"DID YOU SAY SOMETHING, lady?" The force of the accusation buffeted Weston. She hesitated, uncertain whether to reply. The woman stepped precisely one stride closer to Weston. Weston visibly flinched but managed to hold her position on the line. She could hear the shallow, raspy breathing of the two recruits next to her. Or, she considered, was it her own? She watched the middle button on the white shirt before her rise and fall in time to the O.O.D.'s measured breathing.

Suddenly, Weston became acutely aware of the thin flannel nighty she was wearing. Its childlike figures were pastel from repeated washings. The elastic in the sleeves that had been irritatingly tight when new now permitted the sleeves to bag limply around her elbows. Weston wondered fleetingly how obvious the tightness in her chest was. Did it show? She imagined, in horror, twin tents of flannel erupting over her breasts.

Weston's tormentor was now near enough for her to easily read the name tag pinned over the shirt's breast pocket: Hernandez, S. L. She noted that the whistle bore the imprint of warm, pink lipstick. It seemed slightly incongruous with the object on which it was found. Weston could barely swallow. She finally managed a nearly inaudible reply.

The woman before her jutted her face even closer to Weston's and bellowed past her. "Don't ever, I repeat EVER, speak at roll call again." The words were tightly clenched fists pummeling not only Weston, but every recruit within hearing.

Only Weston, however, was close enough to catch the aroma of fresh coffee that wreathed every word. It could have been that unexpected familiarity that prompted Weston. Against any explainable logic, she sought the eyes that belonged to the chrome-plated whistle and the mind-shattering voice. What she found were eyes brown and bright as any child's who can barely keep a secret. The woman's eyes held an explicit hint of laughter before she turned and strode away.

2

☆ ☆ ☆

Weston finished dressing and slumped onto the edge of a nearby bunk. Pain and indecision were cleanly printed on her face. Other recruits in varying stages of dress swirled around, hurrying to complete their morning toilet. She could feel the tall woman, named Yont, watching her from across the cubicle.

"Hey, you deaf?"

Weston flinched at the loud voice. Standing right in front of her was the gangly woman, no longer dressed in her bathrobe. The messy ponytail had been smoothed and neatly pinned atop her head. Her thin arms were partially covered by a worn cardigan, and its matching wool skirt revealed long, thin legs. A heavy wintercoat was draped over one arm.

"Don't go getting down on yourself about this morning." Her voice was lower, obviously sympathetic. "Those C.A.s yell at everybody, and they yell everything." She placed her unencumbered hand on her hip. "You'll go crazy if you start taking it all personally." She sounded to Weston as if she had been at bootcamp for a thousand years.

Weston sighed and looked up to the face that loomed over her. Its grin was unimpeachable. Weston struggled to match it. Her smile came slow and hesitant as if she had to overcome years of inertia. The other woman's smile was insistent. Finally, Weston laughed outright. "How long have you been here, anyway?"

"Oh, I came up Friday afternoon," the woman beamed and extended her hand. "My name's Yont," she paused, "ah, Sharon. But you never get to call anyone by their first name. What's yours again?"

Weston took Yont's hand and felt its rough calluses scratch her own palm, but it was warm and sure against her cold fingers. "Um, Weston," she stumbled over the unfamiliarity of using her surname as introduction. "Roberta, but my friends all call me Bobbie. Where you from?"

"Kentucky. A little, tiny town no one has ever heard of." Yont's answer was a mixture of pride and apology. "You?"

"Phoenix," Weston responded. And then she wondered to herself if people in Kentucky knew where Phoenix was and she added, as an afterthought, "Arizona."

"You just arrived last night, right?"

"To be more exact, it was probably this morning. What time is it?"

Yont consulted her watch. "Looks like six-thirty. We go to chow at seven. We were lucky to arrive on a weekend. I hear weekdays we're up and moving at five." She finished this last statement with a smack of satisfaction.

Weston groaned in reply. "I feel like I could sleep for a week."

"Not much chance of that here. But you'll get used to it." Yont grinned again. "And you'll get used to the C.A.s, too. C'mon, we have to muster in the lounge." She wielded the navy vernacular with relish.

Weston rolled off the bunk where she had been sitting and pulled her coat from a nearby locker. "O.K., let's go."

Yont hesitated. "You better secure that bunk, or there'll be hell to pay later."

Weston stopped and looked from the woman's face to the rumpled bunk and then back to Yont's face. "*Secure* the bunk?" She frowned at the unfamiliar term.

"Yeah, you know, tidy it up. Number one rule around here is secure everything before you leave. Secure the lights, turn them off. Secure the bunk, tidy it up. The navy's big on security," Yont finished with a shrug.

Weston immediately bent over the bunk and pulled the wool blanket taut again and fluffed the pillow. The last thing in the world she wanted right now was to give C.A. Hernandez a reason to pick her out of the crowd. Already she had discovered that the key to surviving bootcamp was going to be blend, blend, blend. She buttoned her coat and snapped her fingers, smiling at Yont who leaned on a nearby locker. "Bunk's secured," Weston winked. "Let's eat."

As they fell into step beside each other in the hallway, Weston could feel her melancholia ease a little. With each long stride she took across the polished tiles she felt the relief that movement brought. It reminded her of the long evenings she had spent in Phoenix as a teenager trying to outwalk her sadness. Even though her mother and father had not lived together for years, when their divorce became final Weston had been seized by an overwhelming sense of loss. She had roamed the streets at night seeking a solace that would not be found but that, after many miles, she had finally earned.

Now that same feeling confronted her once again, thousands of miles from home. It pushed against her insides, making her feel small and abandoned in a large and unknown world. Yont matched her pace stride for stride, and they jauntily turned the corner as one, propelled toward the recruit lounge. Weston's grin broadened until she nearly laughed outright again. Miraculously, there had appeared the tiniest fissure, and she knew it might not take miles, this time, to outwalk her demons. She stopped abruptly and put out her hand to halt her friend. She looked directly into Yont's serious blue eyes.

"You know, I just want to say thank you." Weston's gaze

was unflinching.

Yont met her eyes for a moment and then blushed and turned away. "Oh shit, I didn't do nothing you wouldn't have done if the tables had been turned." Weston could sense the woman was pleased in spite of her embarrassment. They resumed their march through the hallway, grins on both their faces.

The recruit lounge was chaos. It was filled with hungry, questioning women who milled the length and breadth of it like patrolling sharks searching out a meal. They refused to sit. It was the first morning of their new lives, and they were literally dressed up with nowhere to go. As Weston and Yont rounded the corner from the hallway and entered the lounge, a number of the young women who had traveled with Weston gathered around her.

"Bobbie, Bobbie, when are we going to eat?" several women chorused together. "Can you get me an extra blanket? I nearly froze to death last night," another woman piped near Weston's shoulder.

Weston's eyes widened in disbelief at the press of bodies before her. She ignored the swell of voices around her momentarily as she tried to get a quick count of how many women composed this new company. But the mass shifted and changed so rapidly that she gave up. She was sure there must be at least fifty, maybe more. She turned her attention back to the women immediately surrounding her.

There was a tug at her coatsleeve from one woman trying to get her attention. Weston's voice was tinged with exasperation. "*Hell.* I don't know any more than the rest of you." She gently pushed the woman's hand away. "Yont's been here since Friday. Ask her." Weston stepped back several paces from the clot of women and tugged Yont with her. "If we could just have it quiet."

Ever so slowly, silence began to gain a foothold in the crowded room.

"Great, now we can hear ourselves think," Weston sighed. She nodded her head for Yont to begin.

"Attention on DECK," a voice from the rear of the lounge

shouted.

The majority of women, including Weston, had no idea exactly what the command meant, but they certainly caught its intonation. No one moved. From the corner of her eye Weston saw Hernandez stride into the lounge with another uniformed woman at her side.

Hernandez surveyed the room with a critical gaze that left most of the women studying their shoelaces. Seconds passed in complete silence. Weston felt incredibly vulnerable as she stood a few paces removed from the bulk of the others in the room. She would have given anything to have had a place nestled in the far corner, camouflaged from Hernandez' piercing eyes.

"After morning chow, ladies, we'll go through some basic commands and drills," Hernandez began, "but right now, we have an appointment to keep at the messhall."

Hernandez continued in what might have been mistaken for a conversational tone if the assembled recruits had not been able to see her face. "Good morning, ladies, and welcome to the Recruit Training Center for Women." She deliberately kept her face impassive, but her eyes poked and prodded every recruit in the room.

"I'm the company aide, or C.A., to your company commander petty officer Langhard. As some of you may already know, my name is Hernandez." Weston could feel the laser of the C.A.'s eyes sweep across her. "You can address me as ma'am or as C.A. Hernandez. The woman with me this morning is C.A. Winslow. One or the other of us will be with you day and night for your first two weeks of bootcamp, as befits the babies of R.T.C.W. After that you will be under the direction of your company officers and the guidance of your C.C."

Hernandez consulted her watch and then rubbed her hands together. "Now, as this is going to be our first attempt at marching anywhere together as a company, I'm anxious to see how we do. Tallest ladies take positions closest to the double doors in the hallway. Shortest ladies line up back near the watch station at the other end of the hall. Everyone else find a place somewhere in between the two." Nothing happened. Hernandez clapped her hands together loudly. "NOW, ladies."

The mass of women surged into the narrow confines of the hallway. The confusion inherent in attempting to sort out their relative positions led to a rising wave of noise. It reached a crescendo with the strident scream of the police whistle. Its effect was paralyzing, turning the warm mobile faces of the moment before into marble masks.

Hernandez whispered into the silence, "Guideline number one, ladies. NEVER speak unless spoken to by an officer or petty officer. This exercise does not involve the use of your mouths, but your eyes and feet." She paused to let her words take effect, then shouted, "NOW, you have sixty seconds to get it right."

A silent frenzy ensued. The women eventually formed a lumpy, but consistently tapering line from the tallest woman down to the shortest. The two C.A.s moved quickly up and down the length of the line sorting out the lumps, culling through the formation. With this completed, they moved the length of the hallway once again breaking the one line into groups of three.

At the very front of the company line-up, inches from the double doors, Yont stood shoulder to shoulder with two other equally tall women. Behind them, uncomfortably close, were three other recruits, and three behind them. And so it went down the length of the barracks hallway.

"Now, ladies," Hernandez continued, "take a good look at the person directly to your left and to your right. Then, take a good look at the person directly in front of you and behind you," she barked. "No, you don't have to introduce yourself," she spat toward a talking recruit. "Do not forget these faces, ladies. This is how you will line up EVERY time you march together as a company. Is that perfectly clear, ladies?" Hernandez waited; no one answered. "From now on when you hear the command, FALL IN," Hernandez' voice rebounded off the walls, "this is the formation you will assume."

All the while that Hernandez had been giving directions, the second C.A. had roamed the ranks of recruits, adding asides to those in need of further instruction. Not only would each recruit have to follow directly in the footsteps of the woman in front of her, but each must also stay perfectly abreast of the woman to her right. This must be accomplished while marching in step with every other woman in the company to avoid either stepping on someone or being stepped on herself.

Weston felt a trifle bewildered by this onslaught of instruction. As she stood staring at the shoulders of the woman in front of her, Weston tuned into the growing sense of excitement surrounding her. It seemed perfectly impossible that this ungainly, gawky column of women could learn to march together in any semblance of military precision. And yet, there was something unexplainable that she could sense taking place all around her; and within herself, as well. She felt a buoy of hope gently lift her spirits.

Hernandez saw the readiness of the recruits and shouted, "Company, ten-HUT." The lines of recruits snapped to attention in the dim hallway. Hernandez strode to the front of the company and took a position near Yont's left shoulder.

"DOORMEN," she commanded curtly. Two women from the last row of the column ran to open the double doors. Their job was to hold the doors until the whole company had passed through and then rush to regain their places without forcing the company to halt.

"Company, forward HAR," Hernandez bellowed, and stepped out briskly on her left foot. The first two rows moved forward with her in unison. The third, fourth, and fifth hesitated slightly, but then caught on. And so it went through the entire twenty-five rows.

Weston stepped gingerly forward, juggled a few steps, and then found her stride with the women around her. They passed out of the barracks and onto the drillfield where they quickly settled into a rhythm with each other. No C.A. had to tell them to hold their heads up or to square their shoulders. They did these things as instinctively as if they had been marching together since the beginning of time. They looked bedraggled in their mismatched civilian outfits, but it was during that brief moment in the gray Maryland dawn that they became a company.

★ ★ ★

By the time the company arrived at the messhall to eat, Weston and the others were feeling pretty confident. They had fairly swaggered across the latter part of the drillfield. Marching together was easy—left, right, left, right. Sure they had to stop and start again a couple of times while C.A. Hernandez patiently corrected a minor discrepancy or two. But all things considered, they had been pretty quick to catch on.

As the newest company to take up residency in R.T.C.W., they were immediately dubbed "baby boots." Accordingly, they were the last in line to do everything, especially anything of importance. While the senior company languished in the interior warmth finishing their final cup of coffee, Weston's company waited outside. She was grateful for her position deep within the center of the phalanx of women. Surrounding bodies shielded her from the biting January wind that blew across the drillfield. Even so, Weston's eyes began to water from the cold. At the head of the column, however, Hernandez seemed impervious to the cold, hunger, or the frustration of having to wait in line.

Without warning, the double doors to the messhall banged open. Hernandez blew her whistle and called the company to attention. They immediately straightened, locked in rigid attendance as the recruit center's senior company passed in review before them. Seventy-five women in heavy serge topcoats and white gloves strode imperiously past Weston's company. One hundred and fifty oxfords gleamed with a mirror finish in the watery morning light.

Their company flags fluttered in the breeze created by their passage. Later Weston would learn that the red signified the entire company had passed personnel inspection; the green meant the company as a whole had passed its barracks inspection; and the yellow indicated all had passed their final exams. Individually, these trials were not difficult; the navy was determined its recruits should succeed. For the entire company to achieve such stellar success, however, required a cooperative effort of unimaginable proportions.

They streamed past Weston's company strutting their collective accomplishments with narrow-eyed determination. Even if regulations had permitted it, they had absolutely no reason in the world to pay heed to the motley collection comprising the newest and lowest company on the Bainbridge totem.

Once inside the warmth of the messhall, breakfast turned out to be a dismal affair. The compartmentalized tin trays used to serve their meals made Weston feel like a prisoner in a penitentiary. So did the rule of silence. Since you couldn't talk, it made little difference who you were seated next to at the long, endless tables. The food was warm, not hot, and bland. The highlight of the meal was the coffee: it was hot and strong. There seemed to be a never-ending supply, if you were fast. Breakfast was timed to the minute. It was obvious to Weston that the navy was determined to never let the morning meal become an early coffee klatch. It seemed she had barely begun her second cup of coffee when Hernandez gave the signal for them to ready themselves to leave.

The ensuing march back to the barracks was a small improvement over the trip to the messhall. Hernandez only had to stop the company once. As soon as the women entered the barracks, they gathered in the recruit lounge, shedding coats and complaining about the navy food. They were discovering that the only sanctioned place available to them for socializing was the barracks lounge.

Weston removed her coat and immediately slumped onto the nearest sofa. Yont towered over her mumbling something about her pigs at home eating better meals than what she had just eaten. She fumbled distractedly with the buttons on her coat as she talked. Weston smiled ruefully, nodding her head in silent agreement.

"Where the HELL is that woman?" a voice like a foghorn interrupted Yont's lament. Nearly hidden behind Yont's bulk was the smallest, blackest woman Weston had ever seen. She grabbed Yont's coatsleeve roughly and wheeled her around.

"What the hell do you think you're doing on the drillfield,

woman?" Her voice seemed to originate somewhere past her belt buckle. It rumbled around in her chest and then burst upon the unsuspecting Yont like a mallet on a drum.

Yont was taken aback, both by the strength of the tiny woman and her fury. She towered over her but retreated into the depths of her unbuttoned overcoat as protection from the barrage.

The woman's finger stabbed the air in the vicinity of Yont's chest. Her eyes shot sparks that punctuated her anger. "Just because you're six-feet tall and built like a goddamned racehorse doesn't mean the whole company has to run everywhere we go." The woman paused to catch her breath. "While you amazons at the front are only taking a brisk walk, we shorties at the back are having to run like fools to keep up." It was obvious to everyone present that this woman did not relish being made to look a fool. "Do you get my drift, sister?"

Before Yont could even consider a reply, the woman turned abruptly and marched out of the recruit lounge. Like a turtle testing to see if its tormentor has indeed abandoned it, Yont slowly emerged from the safety of her overcoat. "Shit, who the hell was that?" she gasped, as she dropped onto the sofa next to Weston. Weston could only shrug her shoulders in reply.

"That, dear ladies, was Cecelia Taylor," a recruit from the other side of the lounge pronounced. Weston and Yont surveyed the far side of the room trying to locate the source of the information. An easy-going grin matched the laconic voice. "And I'm Amanda Jones, and this here's my best buddy in the whole world, Bev Harper." Jones jerked her thumb to indicate the slim white woman who sat next to her on the divan. She chuckled softly, "And you thought C.A. Hernandez was bad. Cecelia only has one speed. Hot."

3

☆ ☆ ☆

"Attention on DECK," a recruit closest to the lounge doorway shouted. Everyone seated leaped to their feet.

"You're getting better," Hernandez snapped. "Much better. Now, let's get on with this morning's duties." She spent the next ten minutes explaining to the recruits their agenda for the upcoming hours. While Hernandez talked, C.A. Winslow handed each recruit a marking pen.

To Weston's utter amazement, they were told they would spend the next several hours stenciling every single thing they owned with their social security number. Everything: bras, panties, lipsticks, and ink pens must be stenciled before the day was out. In addition, the two C.A.s would be roaming the barracks showing the recruits how to set up their lockers. Each recruit at her time of enlistment had been given an explicit inventory of what to bring to bootcamp with her. They were now going to be shown how to stow their belongings. And Hernandez made it perfectly clear that there was only one way to stow your gear—

the navy way.

The recruits retreated to their cubicles and began marking. Long after she had ceased actually marking her things, Weston's mind replayed the sing-song that had become her social security number. She found she sang it to herself as she emptied her suitcase and placed it in the hallway to be picked up for storage. 529-XX-1533, she chanted, as she folded her belongings so the stencil showed. 529-XX-1533, she chanted, as she carefully placed the items in her locker according to the diagram they had been issued. Weston was deep in thought, mumbling the number to herself, when she felt a soft touch on her shoulder. Lips still moving, she turned to meet the direct gaze of C.A. Hernandez. Their eyes locked momentarily.

"Here, let me see how you're doing," the C.A. said softly.

Weston blinked twice, uncertain she had heard correctly. "Ah, yes ma'am." She ducked her head and immediately stepped back a stride to allow the petite woman to view her locker.

"This is good, Weston," the woman murmured. "You seem pretty quick to grasp and follow instructions. You'll probably have to move some of this stuff on the top shelf closer together once you receive your dungaree uniform." The C.A. closed the locker door, indicating that she had finished her inspection. "Why don't you help some of the other recruits set up their lockers?" Hernandez added briskly. "I'll be back before lunch to see how you've done." Weston was left staring into space long after the C.A. had exited. She had the feeling of being caught with her mouth open when Yont interrupted her thoughts moments later.

"What's up with Hernandez?" Yont whispered loudly. Personal conversations were increasingly conducted in stage whispers between recruits in the barracks. They had been instructed to keep their dialogues to a minimum and centered on essential information needed to perform a particular task. This did nothing to curb their desire to talk and share information with each other, but it had the effect of adding a layer of conspiracy to every whispered conversation.

"Nothing. She said I should help you guys with your lockers." Weston paused, "How's yours going?"

"God, this is so stupid. Who cares how this stuff is stored?" Yont's voice rose in an irritated whine. Weston couldn't tell if the source was fatigue or exasperation. "Have a look. What do you think?" Yont pleaded.

Weston pondered the contents of the locker shelves before her. Yont had done a creditable job of organizing her belongings. "I'd say the placement of everything is about right. But some of the stuff hasn't been folded exactly according to the diagram." She frowned as she spoke.

"I'm not gonna refold all of this stuff." Yont faced Weston resolutely with her hands on her hips.

Weston put her hand on her friend's arm. "Look, if it's on the drawing that way it must be because that's how they want it." Weston shook Yont's arm playfully. "C'mon, I'll help you with your stuff," she said brightly, "and then you can help me organize the others." She began removing Yont's gear and folding it again even as they talked.

Yont simply stood and watched. When it became obvious that Weston would finish the task with or without her help, Yont grudgingly gave in and began pulling clothing from the shelves too.

When they had finished, Weston smiled broadly. "There, easy huh? Now that we both know what Hernandez wants, let's show the others." Weston's enthusiasm was disarming and Yont finally grinned in reply.

"I don't know, Wes," Yont shook her head slowly. "It still seems awfully stupid to me."

Weston whispered in return, "I'll bet we haven't seen the half of it yet. But it seems obvious to me," she grimaced, "just who's going to be making all the rules for the next few weeks." She raised her eyebrows at Yont. "Something tells me it won't be either of us."

★ ★ ★

Before they could proceed to their noon meal, the recruits attended another meeting in the lounge. Hernandez lectured them further on the rules and regulations they were expected to memorize. She chided some of the women for their behavior.

Recruits weren't supposed to swear—ever. It was unladylike. If you smoked, you could only do it within the confines of the lounge, and never standing up. That was unladylike. Lipstick was mandatory. If a recruit was caught without it on, she could be cited for being out of uniform. The same was true for bras. Hernandez warned the offending recruits that soon simple warnings would cease and demerit points would begin.

"I'd like to publicly commend seaman recruit Weston and her cubemates," Hernandez continued. "Every one of them passed their initial locker inspection today." Weston could feel her face go hot, but it was a nice hot this time. She and Yont bumped elbows with each other in their own private salute.

"The only other cubicle that did as well was that led by seaman recruit Kyle," Hernandez nodded across the lounge in recruit Kyle's direction. Weston watched her discretely throughout the remainder of the meeting.

Following lunch they marched directly to the recruit center's storekeeper. There they were given their dungaree uniform as Hernandez had promised. Weston was secretly relieved. After viewing the senior company, she had feared they would spend the whole ten weeks of bootcamp in skirts with accompanying cold drafts blowing up their legs. Dungarees suited her just fine.

They were also issued plain black oxfords. Besides the dungarees and oxfords, their uniform consisted of a white shirt, black bow tie, and a thin navy-blue cardigan. Weston was mortified to learn that the storeroom had failed to order enough of the heavy serge topcoats. After a lengthy conference with C.A. Hernandez, the storekeeper insisted that to maintain the look of uniformity throughout the company, they would be issued lightweight trenchcoats instead. Weston hugged her old, worn carcoat. A thin sweater and raincoat were not going to serve her as well, she feared.

Upon leaving the storeroom, they marched back to the barracks with their bundles of clothing. The remainder of the afternoon was spent stenciling their new apparel. The two C.A.s patrolled the barracks showing each recruit how to tie their black bow ties. It was not as easy as it looked. The central knot should be squared and snug, not wrinkled, with wings on each side that were of a uniform size and stiffness. Too much handling from recruits' sweaty fingers and the ties would be limp and lifeless. The secret was to do it right the first time, and leave it.

Next was their first lesson in shining shoes. The famous spit shine did not actually involve the use of saliva. Hot tap water or matches were used to soften the shoe wax before it was applied to the leather. Layer after layer of polish was needed to achieve the desired finish. When it was acquired, the oxfords were handled as carefully as if they were made of china. The recruits were understandably loathe to actually put them on their feet and wear them out into the Maryland rain.

With dinner completed, Weston spent the remaining hours assisting other recruits with their duties. Hernandez had taken her aside and asked her to help direct the activity in a number of the cubicles on one side of the barracks. Initially Weston had been gratified by the opportunity to assume some autonomy within the confines of the assigned task. But she soon found that it required great patience on her part to remain civil as recruit after recruit asked her the same question over and over again.

For the first time since arriving at bootcamp she was grateful for the No Talking rule. Whenever another recruit was tempted to turn a request for help into a gossip session, Weston adroitly pulled this regulation into the conversation. She had had too little sleep. She had been up since six-thirty and on her feet nearly every minute of the day, without a moment for private recollection. She was cold and tired and somehow she must manage to stay awake for another three hours. Her legs ached and she was surrounded by babies. She fled to the washroom to think.

Weston closed the door on the toilet stall and bolted it. She slid her underwear down to her knees and dropped gratefully onto the seat. The washroom was cavernous, quiet, tiled isolation. Weston propped her elbows on her knees and cupped her chin in her hands. She closed her eyes and tried to blank out the cacophony of voices that filled her head. A tear slid down one cheek and landed in her palm. She tried to stop it, brushing it brusquely away. She suspected that if she started crying now she would never stop. She gritted her teeth and whispered roughly to herself, *You got yourself into this, asshole. No one made you leave.*

Here she was, in the midst of the Vietnam War, safe from the draft in her femaleness. Young men in her social circle at home were having to deal with the fear and terror inspired by the draft notice in the mail. They simply could not comprehend why Weston chose to join the service of her own volition. She had grown weary of defending her decision against their anger, tired of parrying their accusations when she had so little ammunition with which to strike back. There was only the feeling, her intuition, that it was right for her. Her friends had been right, she realized. She was safe in Phoenix, too safe.

At the end of her second year in college Weston had begun to change. She began to question any number of things in her life. She was surrounded by a large, raucous family whose love and devotion to each other was obvious. She had been raised in a small town that helped nurture her through a painful adolescence. She had a mother whose strength and determination outshone any character's she had ever discovered in print. Why was she so unhappy then? What was the source of her discontent?

Weston sighed, shaky and on the verge of tears. She couldn't answer her own questions any longer. All she could say with any certainty was that at some point in time all of these assets had become liabilities. She had begun to feel claustrophobic under the weight of her family's expectations of her. Suddenly, it had seemed as if all their love and support were wed to any number of prerequisites that she wasn't sure she could—or wanted to—fulfill.

Weston's intuition told her the Roberta Weston her family knew was not the Bobbie Weston she sensed struggling to the surface. She had become bitchy, cranky, constantly snapping at her mother and sisters in an effort to give herself the distance she needed. But again, intuitively, she knew it was not enough. It seemed an immense relief when she finally realized she would have to leave. And she was smart enough to know her decision would have to be irreversible for it to have any effect. So when the navy recruiter chanced into her life, she had been ready. It was both the easiest and toughest decision she had ever made.

★   ★   ★

Before bedcheck was completed, before the lights were fully extinguished, Weston was asleep. She pulled the blanket around herself tightly, in lieu of arms that were not there to hold her, and rocked herself for comfort. The tears she had struggled with during the day quietly found their release at night.

She was perhaps four, maybe five, before her father had started drinking, before their lives became nightmares. She still slept with her three sisters on the sofa that made into a bed. In her dream, she rocked with a different pain. Her father had heard her whimpering and had come to pick her up, the glow of his ever-present cigarette a beacon to his face. She hid her face in his neck and cried, "Daddy, my ear hurts." His sympathetic murmurs only made her cry harder.

"Shhsh now, honey, you'll wake the others." He took a drag on his cigarette and began slowly pacing the length of the living room, rocking the child in his arms. When her cries remained insistent, he gently held her out before him. "Here, I'll show you something magic to make the pain go away." She looked at him dubiously, sniffed loudly, and stopped crying. "You believe in magic, don't you?" Her bottom lip trembled in reply. "Well, I'll see what I can do. But it helps if you really try, too."

He pulled her back close to him and took another drag on his cigarette. "O.K., now count to three with me." They counted quietly in unison. And then he blew smoke in her ear. "I'll bet that helped." She shook her head adamantly. "Well, once again then." They counted together, and he blew more smoke in her ear. "It's getting better?" She searched his face. "Maybe?" She nodded her head slowly. "O.K. then, again." He had walked and held her until the magic and the cigarette smoke made the pain go away.

4

☆ ☆ ☆

Morning, and another full day lay ahead. Breakfast was dispatched with little ceremony. The C.A.s had the recruits' schedule timed to the minute, knowing exactly how long it took seventy-five women to line up and march to the messhall, line up to receive their trays of shapeless food and eat it, line up and march back to the barracks again.

Like a beached whale, an old navy bus awaited the recruits on the edge of the drillfield. They filed into its musty interior and learned once it lurched into gear that they were bound for the base dispensary. An abbreviated medical checkup awaited them, and a series of inoculations. The use of the word *series* was immediately suspect to Weston. It brought to mind a gauntlet of nurses each armed with a fully loaded hypodermic lying in wait for the busload of nervous recruits.

The truth was not far removed from her imaginings. Replacing the fictitious group of nurses were only two male corpsmen, but each young woman had to pass between them to receive her injections. The duty of one corpsman was to hold the recruit stationary, while the other pressed what appeared to be a stainless steel gun to her upper arm. They dutifully reassured each trembling recruit that if she remained absolutely motionless, the injection would be painless.

The gun trailed a thick, rubber umbilical cord that ran across the dispensary floor and attached to an air compressor. It clacked on and off at will, never failing to startle the panicked victim of the moment or the other recruits lined up awaiting their own pneumatic executions. But with the exception of one woman who became nauseous from dread and thereafter had to be forcibly held upright, the rest of the women passed through this crucible and threaded their way to the examination rooms beyond.

The first few recruits had been led to their assigned examination rooms and awaited a physician. Weston stood patiently in line, having survived her injection along with the others. Her face still bore the traces of a smile left over from Jones' frantic pantomime of a striptease moments before she had disappeared behind an exam room door. Weston sighed. That woman had a smile that would realign the planets.

She watched absently as one of the corpsmen began coiling the air hose for the pneumatic gun. The other grabbed the handle of the air compressor and wheeled it down the hallway, past the nearest examining room. The one with the hose and gun stopped and began talking to C.A. Winslow. It was obvious that they knew each other. The second corpsman had disappeared into what Weston assumed was a utility closet with the compressor, emerging moments later. He ran his fingers through his close-cropped hair as he strode rapidly down the hallway and turned into a corridor that annexed the first. Something in his movements, his haste, seemed almost furtive to Weston. She frowned and glanced at C.A. Winslow. A movement in the corner of Weston's eye prompted her to check the hallway. The corpsman had reappeared, briefly, wearing a doctor's smock and stethoscope. He had vanished just as quickly into the dressing room nearest him. Jones' dressing room.

Weston hesitated, uncertain what to do. Everything told her to act. Something was amiss. She glanced again to C.A. Winslow. Should she voice her doubts? Should she interfere? Her mind flashed to a summer evening at Encanto Park. She had just finished playing tennis with friends and was walking back to her car. Near the lagoon, she had heard voices raised in argument. As she approached her car, keys ready, she had seen a man and a woman quarreling, silhouetted on the bank. The man took the woman by the arm and began dragging her toward the parking lot where Weston stood. The woman resisted, protesting loudly. The man continued forcing her toward a car several parking spaces away. He finally grabbed the woman around the waist and pulled her onto his hip, half-carrying, half-dragging her into the vehicle. Weston had hesitated and then approached the passenger side of the car.

"Are you all right?" Weston asked, feeling stupid. The woman was unharmed, obviously knew the man, and yet. . . . The frightened woman slowly nodded her head in assent. A stream of swear words erupted from the driver, who had now gunned his engine to life.

"Look, if you're not, just nod your head," Weston had pleaded. "I've got his license number memorized. I'll call the cops." The woman's eyes were wide, unseeing. Had she heard? The driver slammed the car into reverse and careened out of the parking space. As he jammed it into drive, Weston saw him grab the woman's neck and shove her down onto the floor out of view. The car disappeared into the soft desert night.

Weston had not called the cops. The woman hadn't asked, and she had been afraid to interfere. Weston always suspected she hadn't done enough and promised herself that in the future, she would *act* first and ask questions later.

She drew herself to attention and hurried over to C.A. Winslow. "Excuse me, ma'am," Weston interrupted the garrulous corpsman. Winslow turned, irritation flickering briefly across her face.

"HER-NAN-DEZ." The call echoed up and down the hallway, riveting every recruit and corpsman within hearing. The door of the examining room banged open, and the corpsman appeared, doctor's smock flapping, recruit Jones anchored to his arm. He struggled briefly to escape her grip, then ceased just as suddenly when he realized every eye in the dispensary was locked on the scene they had created. Hernandez miraculously appeared from nowhere, and an older doctor strode purposefully toward them. With these immediate reinforcements present, the young man gave up all pretense of flight and stood meekly awaiting his fate.

"Well, Jones," Hernandez asked crisply, "what's going on here?"

As the older man joined them, Jones launched into a description of what had taken place in the dressing room. "This little creep came into the dressing room with his stethoscope and smock figuring to pass himself off as a doctor." She pulled the scant hospital gown more carefully about her. "I guess he figured his white-bread face wasn't worth remembering from the shots he gave us," she sneered at the corpsman. "And he's right. What gave him away was his rush to get his hands on my titties."

Hernandez was visibly furious but remained in control of her voice as she turned concerned eyes on Jones. "Are you all right?"

"No thanks to him," Jones spat in disgust. "Yeah, I'm O.K."

Hernandez called down the dispensary hallway. "Seaman recruit Harper." Harper left the line-up and trotted toward the C.A. "You two proceed to the head of the line, get examined and dressed immediately. Harper, don't let her out of your sight. Got that?" Hernandez nodded to the second recruit to ensure she understood. She put a hand on Jones' shoulder. "If you have any problems or need to talk later, let me know. O.K.?"

Jones whispered her reply. "Yes, ma'am."

"You have your orders, Miss Jones," the older doctor said briskly, "examining room one." He waved his hand at the two recruits in dismissal. Jones and Harper turned to Hernandez for approval, and she nodded her head again, indicating that they could leave.

After the two recruits had started down the hallway, Hernandez turned back to the two men. Her voice was low, deadly. "This little creep's no more a doctor than I am." She wielded the accusation like a knife. "Get him out of this dispensary and away from my recruits," she murmured, "or I'll do it for you."

"Now, now," the older man soothed. "It was just an adolescent stunt. No one was hurt by it." He waved off the offending corpsman, advising him to wait in a nearby office. Then he took Hernandez by the elbow and pulled her further along the hallway.

"Miss Hernandez, your concern for your charges is admirable." At this point he sighed deeply. "This man has a spotless military record. Why blemish it permanently?" The doctor continued, the force of his words willing Hernandez to agree. "I think a good talking-to is all that's in order here." He paused, "And perhaps you could have a word with the young lady involved." Hernandez raised her eyebrows questioningly. "Well, she may have overstated her case just a bit, don't you think?"

Hernandez exploded. "I want a notation in his records and to have him permanently removed from any further contact with women recruits."

The doctor's face grew rigid. "But there is really nothing to charge him with, as far as navy rules and regulations are concerned," he hissed in warning.

"Nothing to charge him with?" Hernandez was incredulous. "What about impersonating an officer?"

The doctor's face registered shock. "Miss Hernandez, let's keep this in perspective. This was only a little joke that backfired," he chuckled. "Where's your sense of humor?"

Hernandez was livid with rage, with the futility of the argument she was engaged in, and yet, she wouldn't crumble. "Anyone who finds humor in the idea of a woman being molested is sick," she seethed. Her barbwire eyes sought the doctor's. "Now, I could even tell you which officer that little shit was impersonating," she spat in disgust. She abruptly turned on her heel and marched down the hallway.

5

☆ ☆ ☆

The wide-eyed recruits still awaiting their own physical exams needed no verbal warning from Hernandez that their duty was to maintain total silence. One look from her black eyes eradicated any need to speculate on the incident. The remaining exams were concluded in record time accompanied by a stony silence throughout the dispensary.

The junior C.A. took the helm, leading the women through their myriad tasks for the rest of the day. Since they were now more experienced at forming and marching as a unit, their time could be more efficiently managed, enabling the vigilant C.A.s to pack the day's swollen schedule even fuller. The final event of the day was the company meeting prior to lights out. Once everyone had collapsed onto the floor or available sofas, the C.A.s took charge of the meeting. They announced they were to begin the selection for the company officers with the next day's schedule.

Weston leaned against the lounge wall and listened to Hernandez with sleep-heavy eyes. "Once the officers are appointed, our job is done." Hernandez included C.A. Winslow in her gesture. "The company will operate the remaining eight weeks of boot camp under the command of the recruit officers guided by the company commander, P.O. Langhard. I want to stress that this is not a personality contest," Hernandez actually smiled, "but an opportunity for qualified recruits to assume responsibilities they might encounter in the fleet. Those of you not chosen as officers will gain the invaluable experience of learning to follow leaders not of your own choosing." She paused to let the information sink in, then added drily, "Of the two types of experience, I'd say the latter will prove to be the most useful. No doubt, it will be the situation confronted most often in your future duties in the fleet." She grinned at C.A. Winslow for confirmation.

The recruits were dismissed from the session just as tattoo sounded from the watch station. Weston sighed. There were now only five minutes until lights out. In that five minutes the entire company gathered around the watch station and were led in singing the navy hymn by the two C.A.s. At the outset this unexpected ending to each day had left many of the recruits mouthing the words self-consciously. The hymn had limped along barely able to sustain itself to its conclusion. As time passed, however, they all grew to appreciate the dimmed lights and the tangible sense of camaraderie that enclosed the circle of pajama-clad women huddled in the hallway. Each evening the song grew fuller and more robust as the recruits memorized the lyrics and, in so doing, freed themselves to sing the song rather than repeat the words by rote. It was a highly sentimental way to bid fellow recruits good-night, and Weston grew to love it.

As soon as the hymn was finished, Weston hurried off to remove her uniform before the lights were extinguished. When it had become obvious to her that a heavy wintercoat would not be forthcoming from the navy, she decided to take matters into her own hands. Accordingly, she sacrificed the top of her flannel pajamas to the cause. By tearing out the sleeves and removing the collar she had improvised a flannel camisole for herself. This was definitely nonregulation attire, and flannelette figurines were all too visible underneath the thin, white shirt of her dungaree uniform. But Weston reasoned that if she never removed her dark blue sweater in public, the navy would never be the wiser.

The makeshift undershirt remained in place day and night. She removed it only to bathe daily and to wash the garment once a week. On such occasions, Weston waited patiently near the warmth of the clothes dryer until its cycle concluded. As soon as the cylinder ceased its rotation, the camisole was snatched from the bowels of the machine while still warm and donned immediately. It was on these occasions that Weston was given to rampant speculation about the possibility of warmth ever existing in this accursed climate.

The lights were partially dimmed in preparation for bed-check as Weston opened her locker door. She hung her raincoat on the corner of the door and placed her oxfords outside the locker too, as fire regulations demanded. She quickly donned a pair of clean socks to wear to bed and struggled into her housecoat. Encumbered by housecoat and nightgown, she clambered into the top bunk. Her blanket was pulled up to her chin only moments before the C.A. appeared framed in the cubicle entryway.

With bedcheck completed, it was as if the light switch also controlled the recruits' metabolism, automatically extinguishing any wakefulness along with the lights. The barracks quickly surrendered to the sounds of the night, with long, weary sighs sporadically interrupted by coughs or indistinct mumbles. Weston lay motionless, listening to the deepening sounds around her, and then quietly climbed out of her bunk. The washroom would lend her the opportunity to pursue her thoughts further without the temptation of falling asleep. Yawning, she shuffled down the darkened hallway.

She nodded to the two women who kept the watch, then paused momentarily before the heavy swinging door to the washroom. Her eyes were now accustomed to the lack of light in the hallways, and she knew that the glare awaiting her on the other side of the door would be especially painful. She squinted narrowly and plunged ahead. Her left arm reflexively moved across her brow to shield her eyes from the glare. She waited just inside the washroom as the door swung shut behind her. There was nothing to do but stand still until her eyes adjusted to the light.

"You coming in, or you gonna play statue of liberty all night?" a rough voice queried.

Startled by the forceful voice, Weston lowered her arm and peered across the room. Sitting on the counter at the end of the long row of gleaming washbasins was the woman who had accosted Yont in the lounge. Fiery eyes scowled through a fog of cigarette smoke at Weston.

"What you want in here anyways?" The question bounced off the ceramic walls, was repeated in the latrine stalls, and again, more softly, in the showers at the far side of the room.

Weston strode purposefully toward the latrine furthest away from the gnome perched on the sink counter. She replied with indignation as she passed, "I gotta pee." She shut and carefully latched the latrine door and then untied her robe sash. She tucked the hem of her nighty under her chin and held it there while she lowered her pajama trousers. Gingerly, she seated herself on the toilet. It was arctic. Her insides froze as surely as if she had been seated on a block of ice. She waited. She pulled a yard of toilet paper off the roll and folded it into a neat square. Nothing. The seat slowly warmed from contact with her body. She used her free hand to tickle her backside just where her spine ended. That sometimes produced results when she was in a hurry. Nothing.

"How the hell long does it take a white girl to pee?" Taylor bellowed from beyond the latrine door.

Startled by the intrusion, Weston yelled back, "Who the hell could pee with you sitting there listening the whole goddamned time." She set the neat stack of tissue atop the roll hung on the cubicle wall. She rose and pulled her pyjamas roughly to her waist, dropped her nighty, and tied her robe. Weston slammed the latrine door open, annoyed at the lack of privacy in the one place she had assumed would be sacrosanct. "I suppose you've been appointed the latrine guard," she grumbled into the cloud of smoke.

The woman calmly met Weston's angry eyes and took a drag from her cigarette. "Now that you mention it, I'm surprised they haven't thought of that." Another puff from her cigarette and she smiled slowly, "Name's Taylor, from New York. How bout you?" The question echoed back and forth across the tiled room.

Somewhat mollified, Weston pulled her bathrobe more tightly about her and shuffled to the washbasins. She hopped easily onto the counter top and slid backward to lean against the mirrored wall. She tucked her legs under her and wrapped her arms tightly about her torso, hugging herself for warmth. "I'm from Phoenix, name's Weston," she finally replied, once she was settled.

Taylor exhaled slowly and studied Weston intently for a moment. "You noticed the john is the only quiet place you can sit and have a cigarette by yourself," she volunteered.

"*Head,*" Weston corrected, "we're supposed to call it the head."

Taylor's face turned to stone. "Honey, I don't need the U-nited States Navy teaching me how to talk all over again. And I especially don't need some skinny white girl helping them," she added vehemently. "You wanna talk to me, you better talk real." She pushed her package of cigarettes across the counter top toward Weston. "Smoke?"

Weston hesitated, confused by Taylor's anger and the obviously friendly gesture of the cigarettes. Would she offend Taylor if she didn't accept one? She considered the possibility that everyone from New York might be like Taylor. Weston shrugged her shoulders, unable to answer her own questions. "Thanks, but no thanks. I don't smoke." Taylor merely nodded in reply and exhaled.

"Are you from New York *City?*" Weston ventured. "What's it like being from New York?"

Taylor scowled more intensely. "I don't know," she snapped.

"What's it like being from Phoenix?" Before Weston could reply, Taylor answered. "Being from Phoenix, it's cold here; being from New York, it ain't so cold." She took another drag on her cigarette. "Why'd you sign up?"

Weston shrugged again. "I'm still trying to figure that out. How about you?"

Taylor exhaled slowly. "Air traffic controller," she replied softly, with a hint of pride.

Weston's face was blank. "What's that?"

Taylor laughed. "Don't they have air-o-planes in Phoenix, honey?" She explained, excitement coloring her voice, "They're the guys who direct traffic at all the airports. They haven't figured out how to rig up signal lights at twenty thousand feet, so somebody has to tell everyone when they can take off and land and what altitude to fly around at. You get the picture?"

Weston laughed too. "Yeah, kind of like a traffic cop. What gave you that idea?"

Taylor took another drag on her cigarette before answering. "My Uncle Roy. He's been in the navy forever. He was int eh City on leave. You know, vacation. He sat there after dinner one night asking if I had thought about the navy at all. I said, 'Thought about the navy for what?' He said, 'Don't be a smartass. Your chances of getting a good civilian job without higher education are just about nil.'

"So, I said, 'No, I hadn't thought much about the navy, one way or the other.' That's when Uncle Roy came on like the local recruiter, telling me that I could get paid while they trained me for a job. He knows I'm smart," Taylor explained, "and more responsible than most my age. I managed to keep my nose clean while growing up in the City." She flicked some ash off her cigarette. "He said it would be a shame not to get some training and then some work experience. We figured that by the end of my first tour I could either re-up or find a civilian job making buckets of money." Taylor stubbed out her cigarette in the nearest basin with visible satisfaction.

Weston stared through the haze between them with awe. Taylor seemed to have all the direction that she so sorely lacked.

She envied her ability to detach her emotions from such an important decision as a choice of careers and proceed with it as though it were a mere business transaction and nothing more.

Weston hesitantly ventured a question. "What if you don't like being an air traffic controller?"

Taylor snorted derisively at the question as she lit another cigarette. "Shit, Weston, you can be unhappy anywhere. Would you rather be unhappy as a $2-an-hour salesclerk at Macy's, or as a $60,000-a-year executive?" The way Taylor posed the question left little doubt in Weston's mind as to what her answer was supposed to be.

Silence enveloped the washroom as Taylor continued to fill the air between them with cigarette smoke. Weston sat quietly enjoying the respite as much as the conversation. She looked appraisingly at the package lying on the counter. There was a certain romanticism about smoking during a quiet moment of contemplation, she mused. But then again, she silently countered, if she just hung around with smokers she could enjoy the atmosphere without ever having to suffer the drawbacks.

Both women started when the washroom door swung open. A plump, rumpled, dimpled woman stumbled through the doorway. She yawned mightily, cracking her jaw with the effort. "Hi. Time is it?" she mumbled, as she pushed open the nearest latrine door. She seated herself, never bothering to close the door and sat examining them through sleep-narrowed eyes, her head propped in her hands, elbows on her knees.

"Name's Bates. What's the time?"

Weston consulted her watch. "Ten-thirty. My name's Weston. This is Taylor."

Taylor interrupted. "That's 2230 for us navy types, honey." She looked for a reaction from Weston out of the corner of her eye as she extended her cigarette package in the direction of the latrine. "Smoke?"

"Sure, thanks," Bates grunted, as she stretched out her hand. Taylor threw the pack lightly to her and then tossed the lighter after it. Silence reigned while Bates selected a cigarette and lit it. She added to the clouded air, lost in thought as she

43

leaned back against the cubicle wall and exhaled slowly. "Now, if I had a beer, this would be just like home," she chuckled. "Well, almost," she added. "Course, it would be nice to have a warm body to sleep with at night." Bates sighed heavily. "Ten weeks without a man. Ooh, I may die."

"Now, you hush chile," Taylor laughed at her own admonition. "The navy knows what's best for you. Besides, after ten weeks of their food you won't know what to do with a man," she added semi-seriously. "I heard they put saltpeter in everything."

Bates jerked upright on the toilet seat. "Jesus, tell me you're joking," she wailed. "The thought of sleeping with that damn duffel bag instead of a man for ten weeks is bad enough," she fumed, "but to think that they'd fill you full of chemicals so that you wouldn't even want a fella, that's. . .that's criminal." She threw her cigarette butt on the floor and ground it out viciously with her slippered foot.

Weston had listened to the exchange between Bates and Taylor with plenty of interest. Having never heard of saltpeter, she was understandably ambivalent about its presence in her food. But she couldn't totally ignore the strength of Bates' reaction to it either. She thought she should feel similarly outraged at the liberty taken on her behalf by the navy. In the end, she decided to take her cue from Taylor whose tone had implied grudging acceptance that the navy was going to meddle in corners of their lives where it had no legitimate concern. It was the price of doing business, at least temporarily.

Weston momentarily set aside these thoughts. "What do you mean, you sleep with your duffel bag?"

Bates laughed. "I hate sleeping alone. So, I cuddle up to it and pretend it's my old man."

"Pretend is *all* you'll get," Taylor hooted. She added the remains of her cigarette to the others in the washbasin beside her.

Bates ignored the remark and continued, "Sometimes I even whisper sweet nothings to it. It helps me to go to sleep." Her voice carried a trace of shyness at her revelation which she attempted to hide by energetically gathering her robe about her and adjusting her slippers on her feet. She retrieved the cigarette butt at her feet and tossed it into the sink with Taylor's.

"Whatever gets you through the night, honey," Taylor snorted.

Weston wrinkled her nose with distaste. "Doesn't your dirty laundry in the bag smell?"

Bates slapped her thigh and roared, "Not any worse than my old man." The warm laughs from her two companions signaled acceptance. Bates sighed and yawned again. This induced a chain reaction from the others. As if cued, each woman gathered her housecoat about her and prepared to leave the washroom. Taylor scooped the discarded butts from the sink and dumped them in the nearest latrine. The women mumbled goodnights as they passed into the darkened hallway.

★   ★   ★

Weston shuffled toward her cubicle immersed in the emotional warmth generated by the washroom discussion. The unstructured casualness was in sharp contrast to any other activity she had experienced in bootcamp. It reminded her of the many late-night encounters in her family's kitchen. Weston had sometimes caught her mother, or a sister, raiding the refrigerator. Then lengthy, highly philosophic ramblings had ensued that were somehow most appropriate to the middle of the night. As she navigated the dark passageway, these memories seemed especially close to her heart.

Weston was abruptly halted at the entryway to her cube by the sight of a shadowy figure looming on the far side of her bunk. In the inky blackness of the small space, it seemed to float away from the empty bunk and toward Weston and what little light existed in the hallway. The woman's gait was trancelike, and as the face became more distinct, it appeared to mouth some inaudible phrase as it moved steadily closer to Weston. Her heart was pounding as the figure moved nearer still and then reached out a thin, pale hand to touch her face.

"Riley?" it softly whispered. "Riley?"

Weston took an involuntary step backward to avoid the

touch of Yont's hand. Shivers ran the length of Weston's spine when Yont silently followed. The thin pale face before her was suddenly bathed in the red glow from the exit sign overhead, which lent an eerie, bloody pallor to the somnambulist's skin. The very same light coated each wiry hair on her head a ghastly translucent red.

"Shit," Weston cursed softly, "you're sleepwalking." Her mind raced, trying to recall anything she might have read concerning the proper procedure if confronted by such a spectre. She concluded the most logical course of action was to try to get Yont back into her bunk.

She gingerly took the outstretched hand of her cubemate and gently led Yont toward her bunk. Weston softly ordered the sleeper into the bed and waited patiently at the foot until the covers settled. Weston stood staring at the shrouded figure for some time, and then bent over and pulled the wool blanket higher on her bony shoulders.

6

Morning always came too early. The absolute weariness that weighed every joint and tendon and caused each recruit to sleep as if she were drugged was never fully purged from their systems. As a result, morning maneuvers were performed by automatons. Except for the clatter of locker doors slamming and toilets flushing, the barracks were remarkably quiet as each recruit stumbled through her morning routine in a haze induced from constant lack of sleep. Weston concentrated on fulfilling her own routine, rushing through some things to leave ample time to conquer the ever-willful bow tie.

Fortunately, the initial morning fogginess was rapidly dispersed by the forced march to the messhall. What exercise and cold air couldn't accomplish was easily finished by the abundant coffee. The return from the messhall was generally a more spirited affair than the arrival had been.

As the week progressed, the C.A.s had been pointedly searching for the company's new officers. The biggest thrill, the one anticipated by nearly every woman in the company with the most excitement and dread, was being chosen to lead the whole company on one of their innumerable marches. It was rather like being handed the keys to the family car for the first time—and the family car was a limousine. The recruit commander was in the driver's seat, and the vehicle appeared to stretch for miles behind her. She could make it go as fast or as slow as she wanted; all she needed to do was put it in gear and step on the gas.

The company was formed outside the messhall awaiting the march back across the drillfield. Once again the C.A.s were to designate an untried recruit to guide the company on the short, fairly direct journey back to the barracks. From inside the phalanx of women, it seemed a simple enough procedure to set the group of women in motion and arrive without much ado at the desired location. But Weston was about to experience the disorientation of being called upon to take control of the wheel. The keys were hers.

"Company, ten-HUT," Hernandez snapped briskly. Seventy-five women brought their heads up, shoulders back, and arms straight down to their sides in unison.

"Seaman recruit Weston. Front and CENTER," Hernandez commanded sharply.

Weston's eyes darted from side to side in disbelief, half expecting to see another recruit step forward. No one moved. She swallowed with difficulty, then dislodged herself from the midsection of the column of women. Her heart beat a cadence few recruits could have matched as she approached C.A. Hernandez.

"Seaman recruit Weston reporting as ordered, ma'am." Weston saluted and then rigidly awaited her orders.

"Seaman recruit Weston, as acting recruit commander I want you to fall in and lead the company back to the barracks. Is that understood?" The C.A.'s eyes were barely visible underneath the brim of her hat.

"Ma'am, yes ma'am." Weston saluted again, turned on one heel and marched to her position at the left of the column leader, Yont. The two exchanged smirks of recognition as they eyed one another from their respective positions. Weston took a deep breath and issued the order to set the column in motion.

"Company, forward HAR," Weston bellowed, in her most sincere imitation of C.A. Hernandez.

Weston's legs were flaccid for the first few yards as she turned to look behind her to ensure that the entire company had cleared the messhall. Once the company was in full stride, C.A. Hernandez began to call out the cadence. It was a marching song only the "babies" of R.T.C.W. ever sang.

"Hip-ho, ladie-O," Hernandez' voice was loud and clear in the morning air.

"Hip-ho, ladie-I," the whole company of women responded.

"Hip-ho, hop-ho, wring out your mop-O. LEFT, your right, your left."

Hernandez sang it without a glimmer of self-consciousness. The whole company answered her, except Weston. She refused to sing a song so silly that it made her cringe. Besides, today she was busy. She revelled in a feeling of sheer power she had never known before. She toyed with the idea of putting the company through its paces: half time, mark time, double time. The words and phrases were savored and tested mentally as she matched the column leader's stride.

They were nearly across the field when she first began to sense trouble. If the company leaders stayed on their present heading, and they would unless instructed otherwise, if Weston did not make a subtle yet essential refinement in direction, they were going to hit a tree. Each step taken confirmed that the tree lay directly in their path. She must give the order. Her mind was devastatingly blank. She scrambled through every command she had ever heard Hernandez issue. About face, forward march, right face, all raced through her head. Allemande left with the old left hand and a right to your honey in a right and left grande. Square dance calls would not help her now. Sweet Jesus, what was the command?

"Yont," she hissed to the tall, grinning woman next to her, "move a little bit to the right."

Yont only grinned more broadly at the panic in Weston's

voice. "What's the command?" she hissed in reply.

All the while the company was marching, drawing ever closer to the tree whose massive trunk signaled disaster as surely as the iceberg that loomed before the Titanic. The faces of women nearest the head of the column were beginning to register concern. Weston knew, as they knew, that the last possible moment for a course correction was rapidly approaching. Each step brought the moment closer, and each step only further served to muffle Weston's ability to think clearly.

"Jesus, Yont," Weston pleaded, "just move a little bit to the right."

"Give me the proper command," Yont gasped, in between suppressed giggles.

Weston signaled her surrender when she ordered the company to halt not more than three paces from the massive tree trunk. An answering sigh escaped the women most directly threatened by the unyielding bulk.

"Damn you all to hell, Yont." Weston cursed underneath her breath as the crunch of approaching steps announced the arrival of C.A. Hernandez from the rear of the company.

"Aw, you would have made a crappy recruit commander anyway," Yont giggled. Weston aimed a hasty kick at Yont's calf before confronting Hernandez.

★   ★   ★

That evening, the fire escape stairwell provided a private, quiet location for Weston to talk to Yont about her sleepwalking. They both knew her position in the navy was in peril if it became common knowledge. Yont was dismayed at the news that she had resumed what she had believed to be an outgrown adolescent trait.

"God Wes, what'll I do? You know when I got to that question about sleepwalking on the enlistment form, I just ignored it. It's been years since I walked in my sleep. Besides, just the way it was phrased I knew they wouldn't take me if I told them the truth. I figured they weren't asking just to be sociable. And my family's counting on the money I'll make in the service." Yont turned imploring eyes on Weston. Her tears were barely held in check.

Weston touched Yont's arm. "Just let me think a minute, O.K.? Are you sure this is only temporary?" Concern colored her voice.

"Pretty sure. When I was little, my brother Riley was killed baling hay. The whole family took it hard, but I think I was the worst. I idolized Riley. Anyway, I started sleepwalking right after he died. The family doctor told my parents it was a reaction to the stress of losing Riley and would eventually stop all by itself. Seems like as soon as we quit paying it any mind, I quit sleepwalking." Yont leaned back against the stairwell wall.

"Everybody in my family loved Riley. But him being the oldest, my parents had been counting on him to help out when he grew up. I never could have said so, in so many words, but somehow I just wound up stepping into his shoes. My parents count on me to help make life for the young'uns left at home just a little easier. And it's something I want to do." Yont paused thoughtfully. "Riley would've done it. So, I just can't get kicked out of the navy, Weston." She turned to look intently into Weston's eyes. "You won't tell, will you?"

Weston draped her arm around Yont's shoulders. "Seems to me it's a trifle more complicated than just not telling. We gotta figure out a way to keep the brass from finding out what's happening until your sleep patterns return to normal. Right?"

Yont frowned. "Yeah, I guess you're right." They both fell silent mulling over this new complication to life in the service.

"I guess you two are still talking to each other," an all-too familiar voice echoed down the stairs from the floor above their heads. Weston and Yont both snapped their heads in the direction of the stairway as the click, click, click of oxfords striking metal steps echoed through the stairwell. They held their breath as a pair of impeccably shined shoes appeared on the metal webbing of the stair tread. Well-muscled calves led to a perfectly pressed navy-blue skirt and starched white blouse. The glittering police whistle caught the light of the stairwell and reflected it back onto the walls and the ceiling; it was briefly outshone by the fleeting smile above it.

C.A. Hernandez passed in front of the two recruits seated on the floor and continued toward the stairs to the floor below. She paused momentarily as she looked back at them. "Don't ever let anyone else catch you in this stairwell, ladies." Her tone softened considerably, "And I won't find you here when I return, will I?"

Weston and Yont replied in unison, "*No,* ma'am."

They both immediately scrambled to their feet and raced for the door. Yont beat Weston by seconds and was gone. "Seaman recruit Weston." Like a child playing a game of statues, Weston stopped abruptly in mid-stride. She waited, uncertain what to expect.

Hernandez waited, too, until the wary recruit had turned to face her. Once she was certain she had the recruit's full attention, she winked and turned to descend the remaining stairs. "I'm not as convinced as Yont that you'd make a crappy recruit commander." She flung the words over her shoulder as she continued on to the lower floor.

Weston blinked in disbelief at what she had heard. She watched the shoulders and head of the C.A. disappear down the stairwell. All that remained was the click, click, click of her oxfords, until that too faded with the closing of the door below.

Weston stood riveted to the spot, silently processing all she knew about C.A. Hernandez. It had become obvious over the past week that her frosty surface was a carefully constructed exterior she presented to the recruits. It seemed in constant threat of melting. More than once, Weston had witnessed a hastily concealed smile on Hernandez' face. And time had shown that what had at first seemed like extreme behavior on Hernandez' part was, in fact, carefully meted out discipline. Weston hadn't been at bootcamp long before she realized that if Hernandez had waited on niceties with seventy-five women, they would never accomplish anything during the day. All of this she knew, and she was still rattled. To be the sole object of such attention from C.A. Hernandez—what did it mean? Weston shook her head to clear it and then turned and followed Yont out of the stairwell. This was another puzzle she needed time to sort out.

The door hadn't fully closed behind her when she was joined in the main passageway by Yont. "What'd she say? Did she overhear what we were talking about?"

Weston strode along the hall in silence.

"Well, did she?" Yont shook Weston's arm to get her attention.

"Huh? No, I guess not," Weston replied in genuine surprise. "Anyway, she never said anything."

"*Whew.*" Yont mockingly wiped her forehead. "Where we going?" She matched Weston stride for stride.

Weston halted abruptly, taking a moment to consider. "Down to the lounge. There's somebody we gotta see before lights out." She grabbed Yont's arm to pull her alongside, and they double-timed the rest of the way.

Lolling on the most shapeless of sofas, her head resting on the armrest, was Jones, her stockinged feet nestled in Harper's lap who was engaged in a silent, intense massage. They both seemed oblivious to the sudden appearance of an audience.

"Jones, Harper," Weston whispered, "I've got to talk to you."

Jones casually turned her head toward Yont and Weston. "Sure, anytime." Her smile was one of genuine affection. "Ooh, you guys should really try this." She sighed and withdrew her feet from Harper's lap, flexing her toes appreciatively before tucking her feet underneath her on the lumpy sofa. She leaned nearer the woman beside her and hugged her, "You are too good to me. Thanks."

Harper seemed to ignore the simple acknowledgment and silently crossed her legs and folded her hands in her now empty lap. She looked up at Yont and Weston with pointed interest but made no effort to speak.

"It's not that long till lights out," Weston began, "can you two come down to the latrine about ten minutes after bedcheck?" She turned her head to peer down the hallway toward the watch station. "Maybe you could come separately so the watch doesn't get suspicious. Yont and I will meet you there. O.K.?"

Jones eyed Weston questioningly, then rose from the sofa.

"Sure, see you there." She brushed Harper's shoulder with her hand as she moved to leave. "C'mon. We'll be late for tattoo."

As Jones and Harper left the lounge, Weston paused to study them. Everyone knew they had entered the navy on the buddy system. It was a program that allowed two friends to attend bootcamp together. Jones and Harper were inseparable during the free time granted the recruits. The fact of their closeness gave the two women the ability to make any space they inhabited particularly their own. This uniqueness was not lost on the other recruits in the company and was fuel for the continual speculation their friendship caused.

Their obvious connection was an anomaly within the bootcamp experience. Perhaps some of the tension surrounding it was simple jealousy. Perhaps it centered on the fact that their relationship was interracial. Weston didn't really know. What's more, she didn't care. What piqued her interest was how two polar extremes in personality had become friends in the first place. Anyone could see why Harper liked Jones. She was bright. She was funny. But what about the other way around? There certainly had to be more to Harper than mere surface value. Weston shrugged. It was time to get ready for lights out.

7

☆ ☆ ☆

Taylor was the first recruit to appear in the latrine after the bedcheck had been completed. She took her seat on the washbasin counter top and immediately lit the first cigarette in a series. She rested her elbows on her knees and stared vacantly into the latrine stall before her. Smoke filled the air around her head. From the corner of one eye she caught the movement of the swinging door as it opened and another recruit entered. Jones moved quietly, rhythmically into the washroom. The two women eyed each other carefully, neither caring to be the first to speak. Jones slipped into a corner where two walls converged and sank gracefully to the floor, folding her legs beneath her. She arranged the velvety housecoat meticulously about her slim figure, preparing herself to silently await the arrival of the others.

"Weston ask you here?" Taylor demanded. "If not, then you better git."

Before Jones could reply, the door swung open and Yont entered the washroom, filling the space between the two women.

She smiled briefly to Jones and nodded to Taylor with a trace of uncertainty. She looked quickly about the room, sensing the tension between the women and not wanting to be included in it. Yont stepped nearer a wall and sank against the cool tiles, letting herself slide to the floor. She concentrated on enlarging a gouge in her rubber shower sandals, hoping to avoid a strafing from Taylor's hair-trigger tongue.

Weston strode briskly into the washroom. She looked quickly about her, taking note of the women present, and hopped onto the counter top beside Taylor. She thumped a wooden spindle of navy-blue thread onto the surface beside her, as if calling the meeting to order.

"Harper's not coming?" Weston directed the question to Jones.

"She'll be along in a minute," Jones answered softly. "You said to come separately."

Weston nodded her head in acknowledgment, silently puzzling over Jones' subdued manner. It had been a long day, Weston reflected, and perhaps Jones was only feeling the effects of it. Weston saw her eyes light up and the life return to her face even before she was aware of Harper's arrival. Harper strolled as casually as she did everything else at bootcamp over to where Jones was seated on the floor and leaned on the tiled wall near her.

"Well, now that we're all here," Weston began, "we can get on with this discussion."

"Yont here," Weston jerked her thumb to indicate her cubemate, "has presented me with a little problem and asked if I could help her out." She paused and lowered her voice. "It seems she sleepwalks. And that's strictly against navy rules and regs. Everything seems to indicate it's temporary." Yont nodded in vigorous assent. Weston continued, "But until things get back to normal, she'll need some help."

Weston held up the spool of blue thread. "I figure all we have to do each night is tie one end of a piece of thread to Yont and the other end to me. It's dark enough thread so no one should see it. We're both on the top bunk. We should be high enough that no one else will run into it. Things should be hunky-dory," she paused and sighed, "except for one thing. Soon enough we'll all start standing watches. There's no guarantee that I'll be around at night to keep an eye on Yont." She frowned and waited. "So, I need some help."

Jones' reaction was immediate. "Sure I'll help, so will Harper." She slapped the leg of the woman standing beside her.

Weston cautioned, "If Langhard or any of the company petty officers find out about this, we'll all be in deep shit."

Taylor cocked her head to one side and stared at Yont across the room. "*If* it's temporary," she exhaled cigarette smoke, "she may have solved her own problem before we even start watch duty."

"Well, we can only hope," Weston said.

Harper nodded her head and added thoughtfully, "I suppose one of us had better make sure we're on duty with Yont, too. It could be just as damaging if she fell asleep while on duty."

Weston sighed again, "Yeah, good point." Silence engulfed the washroom temporarily while the women digested Harper's comment. "Maybe," Weston continued, "once the duty roster comes out each week we can trade around to make sure that one of us stands duty with Yont."

Taylor interjected through a cloud of smoke. "Better make sure it's someone different each time so as not to arouse suspicion."

They all nodded their heads at the foresight of Taylor's comment. She took another long drag on her cigarette in the silence that ensued and then added caustically, "Course, it might mean that you two would have to split up for a night." She eyed Jones and Harper fiercely. "I hope your friendship can stand the strain."

Harper met Taylor's gaze calmly, directly. In blatant dismissal, she turned her eyes to Weston. "I think that should take care of Yont's passage through bootcamp." She pushed away from the wall. "Call me if any other problems come up, O.K.? She walked leisurely from the room. "Night, y'all."

The uncertainty of how quickly to follow Harper's exit played on Jones' face. After a momentary hesitation, she rose gracefully and winked at Yont and Weston as she passed each of them on her way to the door. "Night, everybody." The door swung quietly closed behind her.

Weston eyed Taylor speculatively. Not for the first time, she didn't comprehend how the small woman's mind worked. She had assumed that Jones, being the only other Black woman in the company, would have been an object of the more gracious side of Taylor's nature. Instead, Taylor seemed to snip at her at every opportunity. Weston pursed her lips, about to say something to that effect and then changed her mind. She had enough to worry about. "Night, Taylor. You'll take care of the cigarette butts?" Weston jerked her thumb back toward the sink as she slid from the counter top.

"C'mon Yont," she plucked at the other woman's sleeve. "Let's tuck you into bed."

By no means was Weston's company the only group of women working its way through bootcamp. Every two weeks, without interruption, as the C.A.s gave over control of one company of young women, they were handed another. Bimonthly, a new company was formed and began toiling its way through the ten weeks of classes, drills, and regimentation of bootcamp. All of these women met every morning immediately following breakfast; the occasion was called morning muster.

Each company was aligned along one wall of the drillhall, in strict order of their seniority. The newest companies held the coldest, dampest position nearest the huge double doors. The senior company was reserved a place of honor, slightly segregated from the others, in solitary splendor at the front of the drillhall.

Other than the chance for the rawest recruits to view the finished product of ten weeks of the training center's labor, not much really happened at morning muster. Announcements were read aloud by a different staff member every morning. The American flag and one for R.T.C.W. was paraded from one end of the drillhall to the other, while a scratchy recording of the national anthem deafened them all. The two recruits who carried the flags were accompanied by another who pounded a small snare drum to beat the cadence for their march. This ceremony was designed to replace the actual raising of the flag, or morning colors, as the navy called it in the fleet. Each recruit commander presented her inventory of the recruits under her charge to the aforementioned staff officer. Once the company roll call was presented, all that remained was the march past the staff member on duty, and then each company was free to pursue its own daily schedule.

The drillhall was a huge, airy quonset hutlike structure that formed the hub of the recruit training center. It was the only indoor meeting place large enough to hold all of the companies presently stationed at Bainbridge, but that was only the beginning of its significance. Lining the sides of the drillhall were the offices of the company commanders on duty at the facility, as well as those of the officers who directed the program. All the instructors who conducted classes for the recruits shared office space in the drillhall too. Because of the inclement weather throughout the winter and spring, the drillhall frequently doubled as a gymnasium. For one reason or another, it seemed, the women found themselves marching back to the drillhall over and over again each day.

Weston loved the building at first sight. Its peculiar arched beams reminded her of her grandfather's barn. Indelible memories of summers spent high up in the loft of that barn gazing out over the landscape prejudiced her initial reaction to the drillhall. This prejudice was aided and abetted by the daily presence of a particular staff member whose bounteous buttocks never failed to evoke in Weston's mind the memory of her granddad's mare, Dolly. Each morning at muster, to the forced beat of the snare drum, this Percheron petty officer led the pass in review. Rat-a-tat-tat, rat-a-tat-tat, her buns bulged to the beat. How could Weston fail to love the place, the woman, who gave her what might be the only smile she saw the whole long day?

She loved the hollow thump of marching feet reverberating on the old wooden floor, too. The feeling of unlimited space was in direct contrast to the effect of the barracks on Weston's psyche. Equally important was the feeling that the ghosts of the thousands of recruits who had previously passed through the building and training camp seemed to inhabit the musty air of the drillhall. The hum of energy the building generated flowed unerringly through the well-trammeled floorboards and into Weston herself.

On this day, as the other companies passed in review, C.A. Hernandez held hers stationary near the open double doors. Only after all the other recruits had filed from the cavernous building was the company marched smartly down its length to confront the recruit drill instructor, who waited with arms folded. Hernandez halted them abruptly and curtly introduced the tall, dour woman who continued to appraise them silently. Hernandez nodded briefly to the instructor before disappearing with the junior C.A. behind a door into an office.

The women in the company remained standing at attention, backs stiff with their arms held rigidly at their sides, as the D.I. carefully scrutinized each recruit individually. As the examination continued, the silence in the building lengthened, deepened, became intensely oppressive. The women in the front rank grew visibly agitated under the D.I.'s steady gaze. Once again Weston was made aware of the advantages of her position deep within the mass of women. Each woman in the company sought to blend in with the cluster around her to camouflage her existence under the steady glare of the D.I.

Finally, when the atmosphere began to threaten the recruits' ability to breathe, the drill instructor spoke. Her voice was strong, casual in its ability to project itself as far as circumstance required.

"How many of you have marched with a company before coming to Bainbridge?" she asked. Not expecting an answer, she replied on behalf of the silent recruits arrayed before her, "I expect the answer is zero. None of you have, so relax," she offered. "I don't expect you to be able to march together perfectly before you've even had a drill class."

There was an immediate visible lessening of tension among the recruits. "BUT," the D.I. roared, "I DO EXPECT PERFECTION ON YOUR GRADUATION DAY. Nothing less." She rubbed her hands together as if warming them and finished briskly, "And since that's only eight weeks away, we'd better get busy. From the way you marched in here it's apparent you're going to need every minute of instruction I can give you."

Although the women had learned rudimentary commands from the constant marching with their C.A.s, they now spent several hours learning to polish their performance. The D.I. helped them whittle away some of the extraneous motion each woman exerted by making them practice stopping, starting, and the simplest turns over and over again. As the lesson drew to a close, the recruits began to feel a difference in the way they worked together.

She lectured them about pivot points, voice projection, and the structure of each command. They learned that every command was composed of two distinct parts. The primary command was the function the company was to perform: column right (march), mark time (march). The second part of each command created the timing for the movement: forward MARCH, or about FACE. As the timing was a crucial element in the company's execution of each command, it was the second part of the command that received the emphasis.

And finally they learned about cadence. Just as the easiest songs to dance to have a distinct, unrelenting beat that nearly forces a person onto the dance floor, the D.I. pointed out that the surest way to keep a company marching together was to have someone calling out the appropriate stride each woman should be taking. This could be as simple as a recruit shouting LEFT, right, LEFT, right, LEFT. But a good cadence caller was an artist who could improvise short snappy lyrics around the basic structure of cadence. These songs could literally send a company dancing down a street. The D.I. smiled and assured the recruits that their own company cadence calls would become one of their more durable memories from bootcamp—if nothing else, from the repetition of hours of marching that lay ahead of them.

Before leaving them to the two C.A.s, the drill instructor issued a blanket invitation for any women who were interested to join the recruit drill team. She cautioned them that team members had to rise an hour earlier than regular company members in order to make the time to practice before morning muster. Many women immediately began to weigh the benefits of officially sanctioned time spent outside the confines of the company. After only one week of recruit training, more than a few were beginning to chafe under the forced companionship of seventy-five women sharing every moment of their waking experience.

9

☆ ☆ ☆

Lunch, and afterward a navy classroom. It was in this old, wooden, double-tiered structure that they would spend most of the days to come. They made themselves busy in the cold entryway shedding coats and galoshes. Along the wall, or bulkhead, near each classroom were a series of wooden pegs upon which the recruits could hang their coats. Beneath the pegs was space for their galoshes.

There were no locks or lockers; there was no need. Every item each recruit owned was neatly stenciled with the owner's name and social security number, which made it virtually impossible to take the wrong raincoat, or even a pen. Small things like cigarette lighters or lipsticks were carried, labeled, inside a small, all-purpose clutch bag called a ditty bag. It, too, was stenciled plainly on the exterior, and every recruit knew that it was subject to search at any time by a staff member or recruit petty officer. Unknown, but certainly dire, consequences awaited the recruit caught carrying anything but her own belongings. The navy had evidently thought long and hard about stealing and its many temptations.

Beyond the entry was a wide stairway leading to the second floor and more classrooms. Although the building was just as cold as the barracks or drillhall, Weston rejoiced to see a long expanse of windows on the far side that looked over a ravine of sodden trees and grass. There was even a battered picnic table visible in the distance.

Tucked underneath the stairway was a huge barren room C.A. Hernandez referred to as the gedunk. It served as a lounge and snack bar for the recruits to retreat to during their intermittent breaks between classes. On weekends, when classes weren't in session, the gedunk was the casual meeting place where the recruits from the whole command could socialize. Weston peered inside the lounge along with several other curious women, thrilled to discover another place to escape the claustrophobia of the barracks.

The room seemed to hold little promise other than that until Jones pointed out the existence of a jukebox lurking in a shadowy corner. This caused quite a stir among the knot of women peering from the doorway into the room. When asked about it, C.A. Hernandez grimaced and held her hands to her ears in mock pain as she reassured them that it was indeed operable, but only on the weekends. Jones clapped her hands in delight and grabbed Weston and twirled her around several times.

Hernandez herded the tardy recruits into the classroom where the rest of the company waited with the junior C.A. They were arranged alphabetically, which left Weston far away from the window seat she coveted. Once settled, the recruits fidgeted nervously with their pencils as C.A. Hernandez began issuing scoring sheets. She explained, as she distributed the papers, that the remainder of the afternoon would be spent in testing for the personnel department. She reassured the recruits the tests had nothing to do with academics but were merely guides for personnel to aid each recruit in choosing her future occupation in the navy. She stressed that there were no correct or incorrect answers, simply a "best" answer according to a woman's personal viewpoint and experience.

Of course, most of the recruits refused to be mollified by the C.A.'s words of assurance. Academic paranoia fostered throughout their school careers sent their adrenalin production into overdrive at the merest hint of a test. Weston was one of the few who took Hernandez at her word. She had never been a brilliant student, lacking the discipline for the long hours of memorization the system expected of scholars. But she possessed the facility for retaining odd bits of information that appealed to her restless mind.

And she reveled in the highly competitive atmosphere of testing day, making a game of discovering what she knew and didn't know. Weston smiled confidently at the C.A. as she accepted the scoring sheet. Hernandez paused imperceptibly, a quizzical expression on her face, before handing the final sheet to Yont at the rear of the room. Weston positioned her sheet perfectly in the center of her desk, to see what the questions would reveal.

A petty officer from personnel appeared from the hallway and began handing out the tests. She cautioned the recruits not to open the forms until a specified time. They would then have thirty minutes to complete the test. The recruits began scribbling furiously upon instruction, but after the first few minutes, they had all visibly relaxed. Hernandez had been predictably honest; the questions were easy. At the end of the half hour, the atmosphere in the classroom was decidedly different. The spirits of even the least confident students had been buoyed. But it was only the warm-up for a barrage of forms to follow. The clock ticked off question after question, test after test, the whole long rainy afternoon. They were allowed a brief intermission for coffee and biological functions, and then the tests resumed.

Weston grew restless as the afternoon droned on toward dusk. The relentless rain dripped off the eaves, marking quarter time to the clock ticking on the wall. The questions on each succeeding form had grown progressively more difficult, but the pleasure she derived from the exercise was in attacking each questionnaire and completing it as accurately as possible in the least amount of time. It was this game that held her interest, and she chafed when the time allowed to complete each test was more than she needed. Once finished with a test she had no desire to go over her choices or cross-examine her replies and so contented herself with staring across the room to the view beyond the window panes.

She was thus engaged, staring out the windows, trying to recall bits and pieces of American history relating to the area. A tap, tapping entered her consciousness just about the same time as the Mason-Dixon line, and Weston was jolted from pre-Civil War to the present. She bolted upright in her seat at the nearness of the petty officer from personnel, who stood slapping a ruler on the top of the desk.

"Seaman recruit Weston," the woman bellowed, "you would be better served if you chose to go back over your test forms rather than staring out the window all afternoon. Don't you agree?" She finished with a flourish of the ruler as she turned and strode back to the front of the room.

Weston had become experienced enough to recognize military rhetoric where no response was anticipated or expected. She also knew that now that she had gained the attention of the petty officer, she would be the object of her scrutiny for the remainder of the afternoon.

She stared at the new test form in real confusion. Weston was totally unfamiliar with the concept of "making work" to give the appearance of industry. Long ago she had acquired the habit of assailing each pursuit with all her energy until it fell beneath the onslaught of her enthusiasm. Once an endeavor was finished, completed to the best of her ability, she was then free to gather her mental strength to begin a new project with equal intensity. It was beyond her comprehension how, or even why, a person would deliberately choose to take more time than was absolutely necessary to conclude an assignment. This did not mean she was ignorant of the fact that some tasks require more patience than others, need more attention to detail. But to belabor those details to give the appearance of diligence was beyond her.

She began to fret over the edge of her test form, folding it, unfolding it, ever aware of the eyes of the watchful personnel officer. Weston read each question carefully, too carefully, starting to see words that weren't there. She looked quickly up at the window and then just as quickly down at the test form. The minute hand on the clock hauled itself laboriously past the half-hour mark. She sighed as she reread another question. She heard the soft scrape of a chair from the back of the room and counted the cadence of oxfords hitting the classroom floorboards. A hand briefly, gently, touched her shoulder as C.A. Hernandez brushed past her desk on the way to the front of the room.

Weston watched as Hernandez leaned over the desk of the petty officer, effectively blocking any view of most of the recruits. They became engaged in a quiet and intense conversation. Weston hurriedly marked her choice for the final question on the form and then cast a surreptitious glance at the window. She was instantly mesmerized by the interchangeable microscopic-macroscopic worlds presented by a simple window pane. It seemed to enclose the universe beyond the room for viewing, excluding Weston from being an integral part of it. At the same time, it effectively encased her, she felt, in the room in which she sat, insulated from the world beyond. A specimen sealed in glass for viewing by some giant being.

She managed to rouse herself only seconds before the final bell rang. Weston sneaked a quick glance toward the desk at the front of the room. Instead of the glowering petty officer she intercepted an impish wink from Hernandez. A smile slowly spread across Weston's face and remained there as she passed her completed test form to the front of the class.

10

Following the evening meal and the return to the barracks, the entire company was once again gathering in the recruit lounge for announcements. As women straggled into the lounge from returning coats to lockers, visiting the washroom, and all the other minutia the C.A.s allowed for before calling the meeting to order, Weston sat leaning comfortably against a wall. She was simply content to observe. Some women were earnestly engaged in conversation; some studied the contents of blue binders which contained the week's notes from their naval history class. Others had brought polish and cotton balls and were perfecting the shine on their oxfords. But nearly all were busy. It hadn't taken long for them to succumb to the idea that there would never be enough time in the day to do everything the navy expected of them, nor as well as the navy demanded. Each moment was too precious to waste.

"Attention on deck." Each recruit dropped whatever was in her hands and leaped to attention.

The two C.A.s had strolled into the lounge, relying on their appearance as the only discipline needed to bring the room full of women to order. "At ease, ladies." C.A. Hernandez began once all the women had seated themselves again. "Tonight, just a brief meeting. You'll be undergoing your very first personnel inspection tomorrow morning as well as a barracks inspection. Your company commander, P.O. Langhard, will arrive at 0600 hours and finish before we march to chow. This inspection is strictly off-the-record, simply a measure of how training is progressing." Hernandez placed her hands on her hips and surveyed her audience. "I shouldn't have to explain, though, that it's as important as if it counted for pennant points. Not to mention the fact that the smoother things go here, the faster we'll get to eat."

C.A. Winslow interrupted the short silence that followed Hernandez' remarks. "Go back to your cubes. Either Hernandez or I will be by in a couple of minutes to enlist recruits for the public areas cleaning detail." She proceeded to read a list of recruit names: "Anderson, Douglas, Harper, Kiel, Nelson, Popovitch, Rodgers, Taylor, and Weston are all in charge of individual cubicle crews. Divide your crew in half and send the cube crew for buckets, mops, and brooms. Then get them to work. We'll be by to pick up the other half of the crew for special detail."

Hernandez asked, "Any questions?" Silence. "Fine. You have your orders, ladies." Hernandez pulled a heavy ring of keys from her pocket. "Recruit Yont, report to the utility closet." The two C.A.s left the lounge.

Weston and Yont parted company in the hallway. Weston marched briskly to their cubicle, mentally sorting who she would keep with her as cube crew and who would go on the special detail. She felt someone join her as she hurried down the hallway.

"Weston," a voice whispered.

Weston turned quickly to see who was talking. It was Walker, a small, quiet woman who always seemed lost in the folds of the dungaree uniform the navy had issued her. "Uh-huh?"

Weston responded.

"Don't make me go with Hernandez. Please. She makes me so," Walker looked around hesitantly, "I don't know, nervous. She's always yelling." They both walked together quietly for a moment while Weston processed the request. She had almost laughed. God, Hernandez was the best thing that had happened at bootcamp so far. Imagine being afraid of her. Fortunately, Weston's memory of her own surreal introduction to C.A. Hernandez was still quite fresh. She put her arm around Walker's shoulders as they walked.

"Well, it's too bad you feel that way Walker cause I think underneath all that yelling Hernandez is probably real nice. It's just her way of making sure we pay attention. I guess it doesn't bother me that much because my mom was like that." Weston dropped her arm as they entered the cubicle. "Anyway. Sure, stick around the cube and clean. O.K.?" The relief on Walker's face was all the answer Weston needed.

"Why don't you go get a broom from Yont and come in here and sweep first thing? And Walker, don't forget to do behind the lockers." As other cube members returned from the lounge, Weston assigned them tasks to perform. "You two, get buckets and sponges. Wash anything that doesn't move. Especially stuff like locker tops and chair rungs."

While they went to work, Weston began the process of surveying her cubemates' lockers. When C.A. Hernandez had first illustrated how to organize their belongings, she had chosen Weston's as the working model. To capitalize on the advantage that this had given her, Weston had carefully folded and replaced every brassiere, each pair of socks and underwear, in the exact location from which it had been taken. As a result, she still had a perfect example from which to critique all the other lockers in the cubicle.

Once each woman had concluded her task, she approached Weston to approve her work and so release her from duty. Weston was relentless in trying to second-guess what the next day's inspection might encompass. She checked the locker tops once again, light fixtures, and even the duffel bags that hung at the end of each recruit's bunk. It made no sense for them to have gone to so much effort and then flunk the inspection simply because someone tried to hide something unauthorized underneath their dirty laundry. In the end, it seemed they were as ready as forethought could make them. The personnel inspection was up to each individual recruit, but they all agreed that the first one awake should rouse the others to give them a head start on morning preparations.

Morning arrived and Weston was awake immediately. She tugged gently on the navy blue thread tied to her thumb. Nothing. She groped for her glasses underneath her mattress and pushed them onto her face with one hand while flinging back the blanket with her other. In the dim light of the cubicle she could follow the course of the thread up over her own headboard, across the short space separating her bunk from Yont's, over Yont's headboard, and into the mass of rumpled bed clothes.

"Good, you're awake," a harsh whisper rasped from the doorway. "I was just coming back to get you." Weston rolled over on the bed and collapsed.

"God. Don't ever do that again." She turned her head and frowned at Yont. "I nearly had a heart attack."

"I'm sorry, Wes. I woke up having to pee like a racehorse," Yont shrugged. "It was either explain it to you or make it to the bathroom. After all the work you guys did last night, I didn't think you'd appreciate a puddle on the floor."

Weston jumped down off the bed. "Forget it." She wound the thread into a tight little ball and shoved it in the pocket of her housecoat. "You wake the others." She grabbed her towel and soap, flicking her towel at Yont's back as she passed her. "I'm going to have a quick shower."

Weston hurried down the deserted hallway, the sounds of others just beginning to stir accompanying her footsteps, and entered the washroom. She stepped inside the shower stall the furthest from the swinging door and turned on the hot water. While it heated she quickly undressed. She stood in the pelting stream from the shower and splashed her face over and over again, forcing herself awake. It was wonderful knowing that she had the washroom all to herself, if only temporarily. It brought to mind stolen moments at home when she had succeeded in commandeering the bathroom on a rainy afternoon. Then, she'd lock the door and fill the tub with the hottest water possible and bubble bath. With a good book and a thick towel for her head to rest on, she'd spend whatever time she could steal until a sister pounded on the door demanding access to the bathroom the five of them shared.

She lounged against the tile wall of the shower, cursing the absence of a tub in the barracks. It was impossible to relax completely in a shower. The stream of water encased either the front of you or the back but never both. And having to stand was the final straw. Weston's mind went blank from the staccato beat upon her shoulders. She watched in absent-minded fascination as the torrent upon her shoulders ran down the valley created by her breasts and then cascaded off the swell of her abdomen onto the shower floor. Her feet were scarlet from standing in the runoff. Suddenly, she realized she had no idea how long she had been standing mesmerized in the shower. She quickly turned off the taps and toweled herself dry before tugging on her bathrobe. She raced back to her cubicle just in time to witness the first barrage from reveille.

Chaos ensured directly following roll call as each recruit hurried to give herself that extra moment to reexamine her locker, the shine on her shoes, or the set of her tie in the mirror. Weston hastily surveyed her cube and cubemates one final time. She stopped momentarily to adjust the collar and tie of one of the women before she stepped into the line-up of recruits that stretched the length of the main passageway.

P.O. Langhard appeared, promptly at 0600 hours, with her clipboard in hand. C.A. Hernandez followed closely behind the C.C., prepared to take notes about each recruit's performance. Silence reigned in the cavernous barracks as the C.C. marched down one side of the line of the recruits, turned, and marched up along the other.

On the heels of the personnel inspection came a detailed examination of the living quarters. Still standing at attention, the recruits could only follow with their ears the perusal of lockers, bunks, and general cleanliness. Eyes staring straight ahead, their shoulders rigidly squared, the cluster of recruits standing in front of each cubicle was witness to the dramatic gesture of their C.C. donning a fresh pair of white gloves before entering their cube.

Locker doors slammed, there were a few whispers between the C.A.s and the C.C., and then it was over. For all of their energy exerted, for all of the worry involved, the inspection seemed to be concluded too quickly. True, they all heaved a sigh of relief, but there was an unaccountable sense of disappointment as well. They prepared to muster for the march to the messhall. C.A. Hernandez informed them that the few recruits who had failed would receive additional instruction in their area of weakness. With a wry smile at the long faces surrounding her, she shouted, "Doormen. Man the doors." The two women scrambled into place before the double doors. "Company, forward HAR."

★   ★   ★

Weston sat in the drafty barracks stairwell with her notebook propped upon her knees. She had waited after the evening meal, in her cubicle, until she had seen the duty officer go by on her rounds. Once the woman had passed through their floor of the barracks, Weston knew from previous observation that she had two whole hours alone in the stairs until the next tour. She toyed with the idea of writing her mother. She had brought along the paper, clean and blank, just in case she was discovered and questioned. But comments home would have to wait. Instead, she doodled aimlessly.

For one thing, how could she tell them back home that she was homesick? How could she admit that all the bravado had been only a facade that crumbled quickly once she arrived at bootcamp? She felt the pressure exerted from all sides by the constant companionship of her numerous roommates, and yet, she had never felt so alone. She was constantly seeking ways in which to separate herself from the great glob of humanity in which she was trapped. It was claustrophobic. It was contradictory. She wanted out, but she wanted in, too.

She missed simple things like lying awake and talking with her sister until they both bell asleep. Never in her life had she thought the day would dawn that she missed fighting with them. But there had been a cleanness to their squabbles. It had been possible to fight, get the problem out into the open, and then make up. Weston sensed that even after such a short time at bootcamp there were already undercurrents of anger and irritation that would remain beneath the surface and fester.

Most of all, she missed the sea of affection that she had been raised in and had grown to consider her right. The teasing, the nicknames, and the unabashed moments of real tenderness were nonexistent at Bainbridge. Worse yet, the navy seemed to do everything in its power to keep such bonds from forming between the women in the company. The exclusive use of last names, alphabetizing every activity, and the rigid rules about conduct and free time only served to erect barriers between recruits who were thoroughly mortified at the thought of an infraction. At least they had the excuse of being scared, far from home and any sense of normalcy. She had glimpsed fleeting moments of fear and despair on the faces of other recruits, had felt it on her own, but they all continued to try to hide it. Instead they bounced off each other in frustration and anger, most not even knowing why. They remained isolated in their misery, afraid to reach out to one another for comfort.

Weston couldn't in all good conscience blame the petty officers who staffed R.T.C.W. Although they were the very women who could have been reassuring to the frightened recruits, they, too, were caught in the web of training center rules and regulations. On the other hand, she had already learned there were some officers who were determined to prove their fitness to serve by being colder, harder, and tougher than they had to be. She could only shake her head at the waste. It was as if their credo was, *I'll make it hard for you because it was hard for me.*

She drew a little hangman's noose on her notepaper. How could she tell her family all of this? How could she admit to trading them all for loneliness and pain? Worse yet was the growing fear that this was all there was to life, to growing up. A tear slipped down her cheek, and then another and another.

11

Weston splashed cold water on her burning face. She checked her image in the mirror on the washroom wall and was pleased to note there were few telltale signs of her tears. She splashed more icy water to cool the searing sensation blanketing her face and neck. She was lucky she didn't get the blotchy skin or puffy eyes that lots of people suffered after having a good cry. She pushed her still-wet hands through her closely cropped hair, slicking it off her face with the water. She was bent over the washbasin when the door swung open and she became aware that someone had invaded her domain. A sharp slap on her buttocks made a resounding whack in the empty washroom.

"Hey, Weston," that foghorn voice greeted her. "What're you doing here? I thought you'd be over with the other girl scouts to the shoe shine fest tonight."

Weston dried her face on the towel she had left on the counter top. Initially she patted gently, but then she rubbed more and more vigorously. Finally, she finished and threw the towel back onto the counter. "Naw. I really felt I needed some time to myself tonight," she said, feigning nonchalance.

Taylor's face expressed concern. "Is it something you want to talk about or do you want me to bug out?"

Weston turned her back to the basin and hopped lightly onto the counter beside it. She slid backward until her back rested against the mirror. "There's nothing much to talk about." She shrugged her shoulders. "I feel like I'm going crazy having to live with this many people. We do everything together every minute of the day, but we don't really connect." She added anxiously, "Do you know what I mean?"

Taylor had joined Weston on the counter top, and a package of cigarettes and lighter materialized from the top of her black socks. She lit a smoke thoughtfully and slowly inhaled. She exhaled and patted Weston's thigh gently. "I know what you mean, girl." She paused and put the cigarette to her lips. "Oh, it doesn't seem to matter to most of them." She exhaled. "But you and me, we're different." Taylor squinted at Weston through the smoke as if she had only accurately appraised her for the first time. "And if you're not careful," she shook her head slowly, "that difference will kill you."

"When I lived in the city I saw kids all around me getting into trouble and turning out bad." Taylor rested her head against the wall behind her and blew smoke into the air. "I made up my mind that it wasn't going to happen to my brothers and sisters. So, even though I had my own schooling to finish, and later got a part-time job, they knew I was watchin them." She inhaled deeply, then let the smoke drift out her nose and lips as she spoke. "They knew I'd be there to give em hell if they messed up. They knew I cared," she finished softly.

Taylor's voice grew strained as she continued her story. "Papa worked nights, so I got into the habit after coming home of going from room to room to make sure every one of them was in bed and asleep. Once I knew they were in for the night, and safe, then I could relax. I'd pull up a kitchen chair over to the window and just sit and listen to the quiet sounds around me and watch the street below," she said, as she drew carefully on the tiny remains of her cigarette.

"Watching the street with the drunks stumbling by, prosti-
tutes and pushers in every other doorway, convinced me that
it was suicide to care about any of it. The only people worth
saving were the ones I had just tucked into bed," she whispered
fiercely, very close to tears. Then with swift determination she
ground the butt into the washbasin next to her. "But before you
can save any of them, Weston, you gotta save yourself."

Silence filled the washroom. Weston began her own recital
tentatively. "It's taken me this long to realize how hard it must
have been on my mom raising five kids by herself. Not just the
money and stuff," Weston paused briefly, "but not having any
time for herself. I can't imagine how she could work all day, tend
to us at night, and not go crazy," she confided to Taylor in hushed
awe.

"Looking back, I can see how she was always trying to put
together little bits and pieces of time for herself," Weston continued. "Lots of nights after we had all gone to bed she'd stay
up and play classical music on our old record player. She had
a couple of favorites, one in particular. Something by Tchaikov-
sky, I think."

Weston's voice became a dreamy singsong. "There was one
night I was lying awake after Mom had put us all to bed. Light
from the kitchen squeezed into the bedroom from a crack under the door. All my sisters were asleep, but I wanted to hear
the end of the record that was playing. It got softer and softer
just toward the end. As soon as it was turned over, big kettle
drums were the first sound you'd hear. That night I waited and
waited for the drums to begin, but they never did. Finally, I got
up to see if the record was broken. When I climbed out of bed
and tiptoed to the living room, the record was still spinning, the
changer arm marooned in the middle. Mom was dead asleep
on the sofa, her head thrown back against the armrest and her
feet up on the coffee table. A cold cup of coffee was next to
her on the sofa cushion. I was maybe nine or ten at the time,"
Weston wiped her nose, "and it seems like I stood there forever, hearing the record spin, watching her sleep." Weston shook

her head slowly as she finished, "I realize now that it will always be impossible for me not to care, because of her."

Neither Weston nor Taylor looked at the other. There was no need. Taylor lit another cigarette and blew smoke into the new silence between them. It was an easy silence that held them, comforted them. "I never talk much about my mom, try not to think about her. For the longest time I hated her after she ran off and left us. I thought my dad was a saint." She exhaled thoughtfully, "Now, I don't know. She just might have taught me the most important thing in life. You know, Wes?" Taylor rested her forehead on the back of her hand. "Do what you got to, but take care of yourself." Taylor blew out a sigh. "You gotta take care of yourself."

Weston gently picked up the package of cigarettes that lay between them on the counter top and examined it. She shuffled a single cylinder from its berth. "God, it's Friday night." She eyed the cigarette between her fingers. "I'm no drinker, but I would've had one tonight."

"You and me both, honey," Taylor laughed. "You can put that in your mouth or you can put it back in the package."

Weston paused to consider the cigarette with pursed lips. She nodded her head sharply and announced, "I'm going to put it in my mouth." She jammed the filtered end between her lips and reached for Taylor's lighter. Weston snapped the lighter expertly and then breathed deeply as she had seen Taylor do many times. The butane crashed to the counter as she began to sputter and cough. Taylor delighted in pounding her between the shoulder blades again and again. Weston jerked the cigarette from her mouth and held it at arm's length, eyeing it accusingly. She flicked the accumulated ash delicately from the glowing tip into the washbasin.

"You've got that part down pat," Taylor laughed, as Weston flicked more imaginary ash into the basin, "but I think if you're gonna be a real smoker, you'd better work some on learning to inhale, too."

Weston inhaled a brief moment on the cigarette and suppressed a convulsive cough. Several attempts later she was drawing the smoke haltingly into her lungs, without as much irritation. She closed her eyes against the smoke, as she had seen Taylor do. She imagined she was Bogart in an old black-and-white movie, his eyes narrowed and squinting across a card table in the dingy, back room of a bar. Or she was Stanwyck, shoulders abnormally broad, striding across an old country drawing room with her cigarette holder in her hand. Weston stubbed out the cigarette into the nearest washbasin with satisfaction.

"Does smoking always make you dizzy?" Weston asked cautiously, "and your lips numb?" She leaned her head wearily against the wall behind her.

Taylor chuckled, "Only at first. It goes away after a while."

Weston felt the room continue to spin and the overhead lights grow alternately darker then lighter as she watched Taylor. Like an old photograph, the whole scene had become sepia-toned. Her reverie ended abruptly as the washroom door banged open and Yont and several other recruits rushed into the room headed for the latrines. Their faces were rosy from their recent march through the brisk night air. Eyes and mouths worked overtime continuing conversations begun the minute they had entered the barracks. Their oxfords were gleaming testimony to the evening's labor.

"Hey, hey," Yont blared, as she threw herself onto the counter next to Weston. "I was hoping I'd find you here." She tossed her raincoat onto the heap made by Weston's discarded towel. The door breezed open, and Harper and Jones slipped into the room together, towels and soap in their hands.

"Weston," Jones slapped Weston's thigh affectionately, "you missed a fun, fun time tonight." She laughed as she nodded to Harper for confirmation.

Harper smiled quickly at Weston and then ducked her head, talking over the tap water running in the basin. "I haven't had so much fun since," she paused as she splashed water over her face, "since girl scout camp." Water dripped off Harper's face as she continued, "I was ten then. That's about how old I felt tonight."

"Yeah, but I bet they didn't teach you to spit shine your shoes in girl scouts, Harper," Jones' face was alight with her grin.

"The songs are as bad as girl scouts, too," Yont chimed in gleefully. "You should've heard some of them, Wes. Really awful."

"Oh yeah," Jones moaned in mock agony. "Except Bates' song. She was great."

Weston glanced at Taylor and rolled her eyes disapprovingly. "Oh no. What was seaman recruit Bates up to now?"

Yont jumped off the counter top and joined Jones. They both nearly bounced with excitement. "We were doing this song where an individual recruit makes up verses as we go along," Yont began, "and then everybody joins in to sing the chorus together."

Jones caroled, "The first verse went something like this." She cleared her throat and sang.

> I joined to serve my country,
> but not so far from home,
> and who said it's patriotic
> for girls to sleep alone.

Yont interrupted, "And then everybody sang the chorus. You know, gee mom, I wanna go, but they won't let me go, gee mom, I wanna go home." She was nearly breathless in her enthusiasm. "But, of course, Bates just kept standing there, which meant that she had another verse to sing."

Jones giggled. "They should have stopped her while they had the chance, Wes. The petty officers' expressions were worth a week's pay." She paused, "Get this."

> And though the women in the navy
> I hear are mighty fine,
> they can't hold a candle
> to that man of mine.

"Course the words were bad enough," Jones laughed, but she had gestures to go with them. Bates sure made it clear she had joined the navy to cruise boys and was sick of girls. Jones turned demurely and winked at Harper who had been listening along with the others.

They were all laughing as Yont finished the tale. "Poor Bates, standing there all alone while everyone else just died of embarrassment for her. That was the end of the old sing-along. Who could've topped that?" A number of recruits who had gathered for the retelling chuckled again in discomfort. Bates chose that moment to burst into the bathroom. The group immediately began to disintegrate upon her arrival.

"Hi, guys. What's so funny?" She looked from Weston to Taylor to Yont.

"You," Weston laughed, "and men. I hear you were quite a hit at summer camp tonight."

Bates blushed furiously and began to run water to wash her face. "Geez, Weston," she mumbled into the sink, "the staff here are such prigs." Bates turned her head toward Weston and the others seated on the counter, soap rimming her eyebrows and jawline. "Half the human race are men. Beats me why anyone would want to pretend they don't exist." Bates sloshed more water on her face and toweled it dry. She peered at her audience over her towel. "You know what I mean?" She flopped onto the counter next to Weston.

Taylor's booming voice finally ended the uncomfortable silence. "Well, if it makes you feel any better, I know what you mean." She leaned across Weston to hand Bates her cigarettes and lighter. "Course, some here might be inclined to disagree. Some here might think it'd be just peachy, a world of all women." Taylor inhaled deeply, then exhaled slowly as she spoke. "Shit, if bootcamp's any sign of what it'd be like. . . ." She let her words trail off as she examined the tip of her glowing cigarette, "I don't know. We don't seem to do too good left all on our own. Do we?"

No one felt inclined to answer Taylor's question. "At least men are someone different to fight with," she sighed into silence.

Weston watched as silence gripped them all. Jones' tired face. Harper's unreadable as usual. Yont drooping, shoulders sagging, and stray wisps of hair trailing down her neck. Bates slumped in the corner with her feet crammed in the washbasin. And Taylor, her bristly exterior again firmly in place. Maybe she was right that women didn't do too well when left to themselves. But then, Weston countered her own cynical echo, but then . . . nothing. She was too tired to finish the thought.

She roused herself and poked Yont in the ribs as she slid off the counter top. "Be sure and check in with me before you hit the sack." Weston winked and then stifled a yawn. "I'm turning in. Night everyone."

Yont saluted playfully at Weston's back as the swinging door closed behind her.

12

★ ★ ★

It was Sunday evening, the official end of the new recruits' first two weeks at basic training. With the announcement of the selection of their own recruit officers, they would begin their assimilation into the military in earnest. They would no longer be the camp baby boots. The following morning a newly formed company would be so cursed. Weston's company would retain their much-sought anonymity until the magical tenth week, when they would just as suddenly be enshrined as the senior company.

Even to a casual observer, the change in appearance between this group that gathered silently after the evening meal and the group of two weeks ago was nearly beyond description. It was more than the blatant difference between what had been a riot of color turned now into a duotone sea of white and navy blue. It was more than spit-shined oxfords, or starched and ironed dungarees, or even the meticulous manner in which many recruits sat to minimize the wrinkles in their uniforms.

The palpable differences was attitude. What had been a ran-

dom sampling of seemingly tentative, vulnerable women had e-
volved over two weeks into something radically different. The
acquisition of uniforms, the marching, the shared agonies had
begun to give them an air of cohesion. That feeling had effectively liberated the more timid recruits and allowed them to reach
beyond themselves, some for the first time in their lives. But that
same feeling served to constrain the bolder individuals. They
chafed and fretted under the myriad rules and regulations that
kept them from running roughshod over their more reserved
companions. The team philosophy of bootcamp was, in the end,
the great equalizer. They all knew, regardless of who the officers
might be, that they would be forced to work together for the
next eight weeks. The weak would be carried along with the
strong, or they would never go anywhere at all. And they all
wanted out of bootcamp as fast as the navy would allow.

"Attention on DECK," a recruit nearest the door shouted.

P.O. Langhard breezed into the lounge, clipboard in hand.
"At ease, ladies. Please be seated." Her ruddy complexion looked
slightly more burnished than usual. The two C.A.s who had accompanied her halted just inside the doorway. It was clear that
this was to be the C.C.'s moment.

Langhard beamed at the assembled recruits, turning slowly
so that each woman in the room received the blessing of her
pontifical smile. She fancied that she exuded the perfect propor-
tion of concern and kindness, balanced with the proper amount
of military discipline to "her recruits," as she was fond of calling
them. She also fancied that she received unlimited respect and
admiration from "her girls."

The truth was that the recruits had seen very little of their
C.C. during their initiation into the military. The emotional bond
that had developed had been between the C.A.s, in particular
Hernandez, and the young women. Many of the recruits viewed
Langhard's delayed entry into the fray as a sort of usurpation
of their C.A.'s rightful role. It was little wonder that it made no
difference at what voltage she continued to crank out her smile.
It failed to penetrate completely the determined majority's de-
fenses.

As her beaconlike smile finished its circumnavigation of the room, it floundered on the two C.A.s leaning against the doorjamb. From the momentary scowl that creased the C.C.'s face it was obvious she felt the aids had done their jobs too well.

"Well, shall we get started then?" the C.C. began with renewed vigor. She launched into a wordy recital of the events of the last two weeks, a narration made all the more unbearable by its tone of secondhandedness. Besides, in the midst of despairing circumstances and absolute misery, no one ever appreciates the often-repeated adage that "some say they will laugh at their present troubles." Events were still too fresh for the assembled recruits to have achieved any perspective that might permit a fondness in the retelling, particularly by someone who had not been attendant upon their trials.

This insight was lost on their C.C., who steamed ahead with her prepared speech. It was inconceivable to Langhard that her recruits did not feel about her and bootcamp precisely as she assumed they felt.

Finally, she concluded. Langhard clasped her hands together and pumped them rhythmically to inject some vigor into her flagging voice. "And now, the moment you've all been waiting for," she began dramatically. I think as I call each NEW petty officer's name," the C.C. paused, "she should stand. Please remain standing while I describe to all gathered what the duties of each office entails."

Langhard sucked in her breath theatrically. "Recruit CHIEF petty officer," again she paused, "recruit commander of the newest company at Bainbridge R.T.C.W. is . . . ." There ensued another protracted pause that only served to irritate the restless recruits. She was taking up their Sunday evening, their only evening off, with this silly meeting. "Seaman recruit KIEL." Langhard finished the announcement with a flourish of her arm.

The C.C. immediately tucked her clipboard under her arm and began clapping prodigiously at her self-appointed nominee. The recruits surrounding her dutifully followed her lead and applauded their comrade. Kiel's cubemates beamed. Yont's look of amazement was quickly replaced by a scowl. She leaned over to Weston's ear and whispered harshly, "Who the hell is she?"

Taylor, sitting on the other side of Weston, answered archly, "Langhard's tom." Weston and Yont turned puzzled faces to Taylor. "*Tom,*" Taylor whispered fiercely. "Uncle tom, brown-noser. KISS-ASS," she concluded in exasperation. Her tone implied that she felt she was surrounded by imbeciles.

Jones nodded her head in agreement to Taylor's assessment of their new recruit commander from her position on Yont's right. She moaned, "I hear Kiel's dad is a lifer. She's bound to do everything by the book."

Langhard had finished her description of the R.C.P.O.'s duties and had handed the proud and blushing recruit a vivid set of red stripes to sew on her uniform sleeve that evening. She would assume her command the following morning.

After the announcement of the recruit commander, anything that the C.C. had to say was anticlimactic. Most of the recruits, including Weston's coterie, had little interest in the lesser petty officers who would help run the company the next day. The choice for assistant recruit chief petty officer was duly announced and applauded with little enthusiasm. The master-at-arms for the company was called to attention and failed to respond. Langhard cleared her throat and began again. "Your new M.A.A., seaman recruit Weston."

Yont elbowed Weston's ribs, urging her to rise. Weston struggled to her feet, blushing furiously at her inattention. She mumbled a hurried thank you to the C.C. as she accepted the three red stripes for her uniform, regaining her seat quickly. Yont, on the other hand, accepted her appointment as assistant master-at-arms with unconcealed pride. She was practically regal as she strode across the room to accept her stripes and then carried them reverently back to her seat with the others.

Several other announcements followed, and the list of positions concluded with the awarding of the title of company cadence caller. Langhard beamed maternally as she proffered a single red stripe in Taylor's direction. Taylor's reaction to being named the company's caller was swift and certain: she refused. She hissed to the small group around her as the C.C. explained the position and its duties. "Forget it. I ain't being no token." She folded her arms against her chest, intent on remaining seated.

Yont urged in desperation, "Taylor, get up. You have to accept."

Taylor remained adamant. "Shit. She may as well just say we darkies can't do much else, but goddamn we sure can sing."

The smaller group looked to Weston to intercede. The company as a whole watched the mini-drama being enacted in the corner of the room while their C.C. beamed, oblivious to the passion play going on before her. Weston shrugged at Yont and the others, her expression saying what she could not. Taylor would do what Taylor would do in any given situation. It didn't seem likely that any of them could control it.

Suddenly Jones was on her feet, crossing the tangle of bodies littering the floor between her and Langhard. She extended her hand for the stripe and uttered a softly spoken apology for Taylor's behavior. "We're uh, just overcome ma'am."

The C.C. grasped Jones' outstretched hand and pumped it like a used care salesman. "I know you'll do a good job, Taylor," she enthused loudly, smiling around the room. She handed the counterfeit Taylor the red stripe and then turned her beaming face back on the assembled recruits. "All good choices, fine choices tonight. I'll let you ladies alone now to exchange your congratulations," she sighed as she turned to exit.

"Attention on DECK," the C.A.s called as Langhard turned to go. Once she had disappeared down the hallway, Hernandez called casually, "At ease, ladies."

Jones returned to the others and passed the stripe to Taylor, who frowned in disgust. "Shit, she don't even know one token from the other."

With Langhard's departure the C.A.s started threading their way through the roomful of young women. They were the immediate object of each recruit's attention. Every woman seemed compelled to recite an incident from the previous two weeks together. Central to many of their experiences had been one of the C.A.s.

Weston looked over the shoulder of the recruit shaking her

hand and locked eyes with Hernandez. Always, there was that hint of humor, a dash of mischief in the warm brown eyes that met Weston's. Weston quickly looked back at the woman who was speaking to her. As soon as was possible she moved away, a few steps closer to the center of the room, and Hernandez. She must talk to her. She was ambushed by another recruit.

"I just knew that you'd get picked to be one of the officers," the woman shook Weston's hand. Weston nodded in reply and looked quickly again toward Hernandez. Her back was turned, her head bent as she listened to another recruit's tale.

Weston was torn. Part of her said she should rush across the room and blurt out how much Hernandez had come to mean to her, how much she was going to miss the humor with which Hernandez defused so many situations. Another part of her said no, that was how babies acted. Hernandez went to great lengths to construct and maintain a tough exterior that said she was all business. Just doing her job. Taylor, too, went about life encased in armorplate. It was time that she, Weston, grew up and quit wearing her heart on her sleeve. Besides, the pouty, petulant side of her argued, it was she who was being left, not Hernandez. Let Hernandez do the gushing, this other self whined.

Reason had no part in these thrusts and counterthrusts that Weston parried within herself. It made not a whit of difference that it had been clear from the beginning that the C.A.'s job encompassed only the first two weeks of bootcamp. Weston could not fight her feeling of abandonment with logic. She had come to rely on Hernandez, and the feeling of being cast adrift too soon was overwhelming.

And yet it seemed wrong not to take Hernandez aside and attempt to explain how much she had given. Even though much of the gift was still cloaked in mystery for Weston, she couldn't ignore the feeling that a door had been opened for her. It was more than Hernandez' humor, her thinly veiled cynicism about the military. That humor had given her the foothold she needed to pull herself free of the military's great narcotic—power. But there was more, something undefinable. And even if Weston couldn't put it into words, she must at least shake Hernandez' hand. Weston searched the women's faces in the center of the room. Hernandez was gone.

Part Two
☆ ☆ ☆
SERVICE WEEK

13

Weston's internal alarm system jolted her awake. She lay motionless for some moments trying to recall the exact reason for this sudden arousal. She blinked her eyes rapidly, pushing aside sleepiness, then untied the thread on her thumb and rubbed her face with the palms of her hands. She fumbled for her eyeglasses. Weston folded her hands behind her head and focused on the darkness above her bunk. The mid-watch would appear at any moment to awaken her.

"Sst," a voice hissed in her ear. "Weston, R. D., are you awake?" Navy rules and regulations prohibited the watchstander from actually touching Weston. She could call her. Or, if that failed she could shine a flashlight in her face. But never, under any circumstances, was the watchstander allowed to touch another recruit who was in her bunk.

Weston turned onto her side to allow herself to see the other woman's face before she answered. "Yeah, I'm awake. What time is it?"

The watchstander shone her flashlight on her wristwatch. "Zero four hundred hours," she replied. "The fire drill commences in ten minutes," she added. "Your R.C.P.O. said to tell you to be ready for a long night."

"What the hell does that mean?" Weston asked angrily. "A fire drill's a fire drill, isn't it?"

The watchstander shrugged. "So are you up?" she whispered after Weston had made no effort to move.

Weston groaned as she threw off the wool blanket. "Yeah, I'm up, I'm up. See?" She slowly clambered down from the top bunk. Only when her feet had touched the floor did the other woman turn to leave the cubicle. Weston threw her hands over her head and stretched vigorously. She then slipped her stockinged feet into her oxfords. Tying them quickly, she reached for her overcoat. She paused before donning it and reconsidered the watchstander's message. She tugged off her shoes and hastily pulled on her trousers, shirt, and sweater before pulling the overcoat on again. Weston quickly straightened the blanket on her bed and then fled down the dim hallway to the washroom. As she ran she scrambled to check that the pocket of her raincoat still held the flashlight she had been issued the evening before.

The officers of the company had been forewarned that the fire drill would take place early on this Saturday morning. They had been briefed as to the nature of their duties. The R.C.P.O. was to lead the company down the designated fire exit and out onto the grinder. Once the full company had assembled, she would commence roll call. Her final duty was to inform the recruits under her command of the time that had elapsed since the drill began. As the company M.A.A. it was Weston's task to ensure that every cube was searched, that every recruit on their floor exited the building.

Weston quickly inspected the massive washroom and then strode across the hallway to check the lounge. As anticipated, both proved to be empty. She then hurried past the watch station to take up a position at the opposite end of the barracks from their exit. She would make a thorough search of every bunk before she made her own exit.

Pandemonium reigned once the alarm sounded. Even though she had been alerted to its occurrence, Weston was nearly swept away in the bedlam that resulted. Few others had been made aware of the early morning rehearsal in order to more accurately assess the recruits' reactions and timing. Understandably, many bleary-eyed women assumed the call was reveille. They dutifully began lining up outside their cubicles for roll call. The assistant R.C.P.O. patrolled the passageways urging these sleepyheads to don their overcoats and oxfords and join the exodus through the fire exit.

Weston undertook her systematic search of each of the cubicles as the barracks began to empty. The blaring fire alarm continued to dredge up panic in her soul. Her heart pounded, and she had to continually remind herself that this was, after all, only a drill. The temptation to not search fully was almost overwhelming in her eagerness to be out from under the screaming siren.

In the midst of searching one of the last cubicles, Weston halted abruptly when she distinctly heard the clang of the fire exit door slam shut. The last recruit had filed out to safety, and she was now alone with her escalating panic in the dimly lit barracks. The siren continued its demolition of the once quiet night. Her breath began to come in short, sharp gasps. She imagined the beam of the flashlight had begun to flicker. It took all of her willpower to force herself to finish the search of that final cubicle. Then, as she probed the bunched bedclothes of the last bunk with one hand, Weston's body was beginning the pivot that propelled her to the exit door. She flung the heavy door open and flew down the fire escape. She leapt the two remaining stairs and crashed through the second metal door, hurtling into the night.

Her company was arranged in formation on the drillfield. Of all the companies that had so recently exited the barracks they were, without a doubt, the sorriest lot. Many of the recruits had forgotten their overcoats in their panic. A few wore slippers instead of their oxfords. All of them shivered uncontrollably, as much from the adrenalin that had flooded their systems as the cold night air. Weston composed herself enough to make a hurried report to Kiel, who was immaculately dressed as usual. Weston saluted and then gratefully assumed her usual position in the midst of the company line-up.

Kiel pivoted expertly on one foot and rigidly strode the three paces to repeat Weston's report to the C.C. Then Langhard made a careful notation on her ever-present clipboard and spoke a few quiet words to the attentive R.C.P.O. A crisp salute and Kiel turned again, marching the few paces back to the front rank of the company. Beside her the mass of shivering recruits eyed their company commander woefully.

A similar scene was being enacted across the grinder as the other C.C.s received their reports. Langhard let her recruits stand and wait. She let them listen as the first of the other recruits marched off the field and back to the warm barracks. Still she waited without a word, the expression on her face indecipherable. A growing melancholy embraced the recruits as they listened to the rasping footsteps of the last company marched off the grinder. "Left, left, left." The cadence call grew softer and softer until it was only a whisper, and then no more.

"FIVE minutes, ladies," Langhard began. Her small eyes seemed to spear the line of recruits nearest her. Her stubby forefinger jabbed the air once, twice, three times branding individual recruits as she spoke. "YOU, you, and you," she bellowed, "are DEAD. Killed by your own and your fellow recruits' dawdling. Dead from smoke inhalation." She promptly culled five more women from the forlorn group. "You five are all badly burned and will have to be taken to the hospital simply because you failed to follow proper procedure. Tonight you were lucky. You're only a little cold because you forgot to don your overcoats and oxfords, per instructions. The next time," she paused, "well, there won't be a next time quite like this. Will there, ladies?" The whole company wilted even more dramatically under their C.C.'s onslaught.

Langhard continued softly, almost apologetically. "The worst of it is that in failing to follow orders, you may be simply inconvenienced or injured," she paused significantly, "but your company M.A.A. is dead as well." Weston flinched as if she had been struck. "Dead because SHE obeyed her orders. Her duty was to be the last out of the barracks. And each and every one of you who was slow or unprepared tonight have helped to write her epitaph." There followed an extended moment of silence. Weston could only assume it was for their fallen, but dutiful, M.A.A.

The C.C. exploded anew at the exhausted recruits. "IN the time it took this company to exit the barracks, if there had indeed been a fire, your M.A.A., your A.R.C.P.O., and the three recruits that preceded them would all be history right now, ladies." She paused, "TOAST, if you get my meaning." The C.C. snapped her clipboard down to her side to emphasize her final statement.

"Kiel, front and center," Langhard growled. The R.C.P.O. brought herself to attention and then strode to the front of the company, stopping directly before the company commander. "Take this sorry lot back into the barracks and start the drill over," the C.C. said contemptuously. The cold night air condensed around her words and turned them into puffs of vapor that fell soddenly to the ground. "And do it," she added, "until they get it right." Before her words had finished echoing in the night, the C.C. had turned on her heel and strode away.

Kiel executed a crisp salute to the departing commander's back in acknowledgement of the order. She then turned to face the weary recruits. "Well," she eyed them thoughtfully, savoring the moment, then pronouncing with obvious relish, "you heard the command. Drill until we get it right. Company, ten-HUT," Kiel thundered. Seventy-four women grudgingly brought themselves to attention. Kiel's eyes narrowed in irritation at their slow response. "Ladies," she said softly, "if this takes all night, you have no one to blame but yourselves. Now, let's get on with it."

"Company, right FACE," she ordered. The overall response was devoid of enthusiasm but appreciably faster. Kiel seemed content to accept this partial victory of will, for the time being. As they began the march back across the deserted drillfield to the barracks, she made careful mental notes of who appeared ready to cooperate that night and who didn't.

And they drilled until reveille sounded, until daybreak interceded where the R.C.P.O.'s conscience would not.

14

☆ ☆ ☆

"It's beyond me why you always choose to smoke in here instead of the lounge," Weston said, as she slid to the washroom floor to sit beside Taylor. She threw back her head and yawned mightily before continuing, "You know it's against the regs."

Taylor turned and eyed Weston silently. It was some moments before she offered Weston her package of cigarettes, "Wanna smoke?"

Weston yawned again, "Yeah, I guess so." She carefully withdrew one cigarette, leaving the package in Taylor's outstretched hand. She lit it and took a few hesitant puffs. Weston managed to inhale without an immediate wracking cough, so she exhaled quickly and attempted a longer, deeper drag. Through painful trial and error Weston had discovered that if she inhaled slowly, very slowly, she could actually finish a whole cigarette without coughing. She had resigned herself to never achieving the easy nonchalance with which Taylor dispatched each one.

"Well, I'll try and explain it to you," Taylor began, as she rested one arm on her bent knee. "Smoking can be a social experience at times, right?" Weston nodded her head in agreement. "Now, think Weston, which recruits only smoke in the lounge?" Taylor questioned softly. "And which recruits could give a shit about all the petty rules and regulations the navy tries to lay on us and smoke in the washroom?" Weston attempted to answer, but was silenced by Taylor's raised hand. "No, wait. Here comes the hard part. Of the aforementioned recruits, who do *you* think I would rather share a social experience with, oh dutiful M.A.A.?"

Weston sighed as she exhaled the final drag on her cigarette. "As usual, Taylor, you have gotten to the heart of the matter light years ahead of me." Taylor merely nodded her head in mute acknowledgment. Neither of the women seemed possessed of the energy to continue their teasing. They willingly pulled the cold-tiled silence of the empty washroom around themselves. The plumbing gurgled and groaned, and the glare from the overhead lights burned their tired eyes, but they were momentarily alone. And that felt good.

Later they were quietly joined by Harper and Jones, who appeared silently, as if by magic. They seemed not the least bit surprised to find Taylor and Weston seated on the washroom floor, unspeaking. They entered the soundless circle like bathers entering a thermal pool. Harper leaned comfortably against the icy wall, her thin shoulder blades bearing the brunt of her weight. Smokes and a lighter materialized from underneath her trouser leg. Jones slid to the floor opposite the already-seated recruits. She immediately began pulling cotton balls, a can of black shoe polish, and a lighter from her ditty bag. She untied her oxfords and removed them from her feet, then shifted her weight from right cheek to left and tucked her feet into the bends of her knees for warmth. Once Jones was comfortably settled, she reached for a shoe, selected a cotton ball, spit on it, and began to wipe the surface dust from it.

"Cigarette?" Taylor asked dreamily, extending her package toward Jones.

Jones smiled in reply. "No thanks." She began to hum softly to herself as she became involved in the process of shining her shoes. She flicked the butane lighter to life and held the can of shoe polish over the flame. The portion of the solid polish heated by the flame grew soft, then molten. Jones snapped the lighter lid closed and grabbed a clean cotton ball. She scooped up the nearly liquid polish and began to apply it to her oxford. Gently, round and round and round, she circle-swabbed the polish to the leather until every millimeter of it had been covered.

Once the shoe had been coated in warm polish, she could begin the second step in achieving the mirrorlike finish on her oxfords. Another cotton ball was soaked in the hottest water possible and then all the water squeezed out. It was absolutely essential to begin rubbing the polished shoe while the cotton ball was barely cool enough to touch. It was this second application of heat that glazed the surface polish over the saturated pores of the leather. This painstaking effort produced a finish in which a diligent recruit could quite literally see the reflection of her own features. The final touch was to take a soft cloth and buff the leather lightly to enhance the shine.

Jones caught Weston's eye and then slid the can of polish across the floor to her. Weston responded by removing her own oxfords and reaching for a cotton ball to dust them with. Harper eased herself away from the wall and fully joined the circle of women. The motion, sensual and fluid, as Harper's slight frame folded and settled on the cold tile opposite Weston, diverted her attention away from the shoe she scrubbed. Thoughtful green eyes met Weston's gaze.

At this late hour it was not unusual for Weston's head to reel from too little sleep, cigarette smoke, and tonight, what else? What was she seeing in Harper's eyes? Somehow, she felt it was herself. Herself reflected, herself beheld. Harper's eyes seemed to say quite clearly, "I know you." Weston had no inkling of what her eyes said in return. She forced her attention back to the shoe in her hand. She had learned to like this woman and the quiet way she dealt with life. Suddenly the washroom seemed unbearably hot to Weston, and she could no longer tolerate the close confines of the circle.

She rose, crossed the room to the toilet stalls, and flushed away the remains of her cigarette. She moistened several cotton balls at the nearest sink before returning to her seat next to Taylor. The small woman resettled herself adroitly to make more room for Weston and then ground out a butt on the floor between them. Taylor reached for the cotton balls in the center of the circle as well. Weston grimaced theatrically at Taylor's habit of butting her cigarettes wherever she happened to be sitting.

As the company M.A.A. she could not witness such flagrant violations of the regs without registering some comment. But as Taylor's friend, Weston silently applauded her continuing defiance of the status quo. The problem was that it left her feeling like she inhabited two worlds.

One was the world of the company petty officers and their innumerable meetings. At first, Kiel was hesitant, almost ingratiating in the way she commanded the women in the company. But as she became more certain of her power through Langhard's backing, Kiel's treatment of the group was increasingly relentless. Her uncompromising attitude created a chasm that divided the whole company. Half the women became spit-and-polish automatons who jumped at Kiel's every suggestion. The other half of the great divide was populated by a variety of smaller factions whose only common denominator seemed to be their dislike for the R.C.P.O.

The polarization happened so quickly that it had, in all probability, been inevitable. Weston sighed audibly as she continued to shine her oxfords. The upshot was that she often seemed to be occupying the only determinedly neutral position. She was constantly reminded of the precariousness of this terrain. As the third-ranking officer in the company, Weston knew that Kiel expected her support but continually suspected her allegiance. Weston was certain she would have been replaced if it weren't for the fact that no one else wanted her job. Master-at-arms of the company quarters was much like a dorm mother's job: twenty-four-hour surveillance on the communal neatness of all the women under her command.

And there was the little matter of the dreary woman who was the master-at-arms of the entire recruit barracks. Three floors, nearly five hundred women, and the scuttlebutt was that Weston was one of her favorites. This did not mean that she yelled any less at Weston, or her assistant, Yont. What it did mean was that the company had never yet completely flunked an inspection, although they had been close. So Kiel was resigned to keeping Weston on as the company M.A.A.

The others, including Taylor, seemed to demand incessant proof of Weston's neutrality, if not her outright support. Weston had been ready to resign her post late in the third week after a particularly contentious officers' meeting. It was Taylor who convinced her to stay. Weston appraised the flattened butt on the floor. Taylor had talked her into remaining as the M.A.A. and then continued her small exploitations of the company rules and regs to the point where Weston sometimes felt on the brink of tears with exasperation.

If her support at officers' meetings was so important to Taylor, why didn't she make life outside those meetings any easier? Weston could sense an inner battle raging in Taylor and felt that the woman couldn't, or wouldn't, communicate its source. Instead, Taylor pushed and prodded and probed and then pretended to be oblivious to Weston's reactions. Weston shook her head in disbelief at the woman seated next to her. There were times when the anger she generated was palpable. But Weston had finally come to trust that although it might color the boundaries of their friendship, it would not be directed at her.

15

★ ★ ★

"Hey, Weston. Me and Harper are going over to the gedunk," Jones shouted from the hallway. "You gonna come?"

Weston looked up abruptly from her notes on naval history. A smile spread slowly across her face as she focused her
attention on the woman slouched in the entryway of the cubicle.
Jones raised her eyebrows, repeating the question with the motion. "C'mon. The others are already over there waiting for us."

"God, I'm not feeling that well," Weston paused, "and I really
should study this history crap for our test." She suddenly snapped
her binder shut. "But sure. Great. Just give me five minutes to
get ready, O.K.?" She rose from the bunk on which she had
been seated. "I'll meet you in the lounge." Weston automatically smoothed the depression in the pillow and blanket. She
looked up in time to catch an amiable salute from the departing
recruit.

Weston carefully replaced her binder in its allotted place
inside her locker, then diligently scanned the cubicle while don-

ning her overcoat and cap. Part of her resented this constant checking and rechecking to ensure that everything was in its place. It was military busywork at its best. But she also felt she couldn't ask the rest of the company to follow rules she didn't follow herself, so she tidied until it became second nature, until she could do it in her sleep. She sometimes took it personally that her efforts met with only measured success. Her cubemates were wonderful. Initially, they had merely humored her simply because of her intense desire to do the job of M.A.A. as well as possible. Weston knew it was solely because they hadn't cared at all that they had let her shepherd them into conformity with her wishes.

Once several inspections passed and theirs was one of the few cubes to have survived each ordeal without demerit points, Weston began to notice a subtle change in their attitudes. They all began to exude a proprietary air toward the general appearance of the cubicle. This manifested itself in more consistent individual efforts. Weston simply didn't have to bug them as much. It hadn't been quite that straightforward with the rest of the company. Other than a few outstanding exceptions, most of the women seemed content to do just enough to get by.

But they all appeared to have developed incredible intuition regarding the arrival of the officer on duty. This R.T.C.W. staff member patrolled each floor every two hours. Every recruit knew that the barracks and cubicles should be ready for a snap inspection any time of the day. And they would have been if the rules were followed. Instead, wholesale petty mutiny occurred between the rotation of the watch. And then, mere seconds before the appearance of the O.O.D. walking her rounds, a radical change would sweep through the barracks. The most vehement of quarrels stopped midsentence. Cigarettes were stubbed out and the air fanned energetically by every recruit in sight, not just the smokers. It was a perverse pool of fellowship that existed at these moments, and Weston wished dearly that she knew the secret of how to tap into it. The feeling was like dry ice: it was tangible one moment and then disappeared into nothing along with the O.O.D. the minute the door closed behind her. Weston shrugged in resignation.

She passed the laundry room and paused to give it a quick look. A recruit's shirt, cold and rumpled, lay in the dryer. She noted the name printed on the inside of the collar and draped it over her arm while she checked the lint trap at the bottom of the machine. Predictably, it was lined with fluff. No one seemed capable of remembering to empty it either before or after using the dryer. A blue notebook lay abandoned on the ironing board. She flipped it open to look for the name and then resumed her march down the passageway. Weston dropped the notebook on a bunk in a cubicle nearest the laundry room. She then proceeded along the hallway and found the recruit she was seeking leaning over a bunk railing, deep in conversation. Weston tossed the shirt toward the two women.

"It'll take you forever to get the wrinkles out of this sucker."

"The closest woman smiled at Weston as she caught the garment. "Where you headed?"

"Gedunk. I can't spend all of Saturday afternoon studying." Weston added with mock severity, "I'll send you my bill at the end of the month for picking up after you." She was still smiling when she passed Kiel coming out of the recruit lounge.

"Who were you picking up after, now? How many points did you give them?" Kiel demanded, stopping Weston in the hallway.

Weston sighed as she reluctantly came to a halt opposite the R.C.P.O. "Nobody. Nothing. It's Saturday, and I'm off duty." Weston's smile faded as she met the eyes of the woman across from her. "C'mon Kiel. I really don't want to get into this." It was common knowledge among the company officers that Kiel thought Weston was too easy on everyone. Their arguments about demerit points were numerous and seemingly circular.

"Look, if you want to spend all your free time picking up these ladies' socks and undergarments," Kiel shrugged, "it's a little kinky, but it's your business. Have you ever stopped to consider what's going to happen to them after they leave bootcamp though?"

Weston snorted in disbelief at Kiel's question. "I don't know," she paused, "they'll find kinky boyfriends or husbands who'll do it for them. That'd be a nice role reversal, don't you think?"

Kiel frowned. "You're missing my point on purpose, Weston. We're here to teach these ladies how to follow orders, how to carry out specific tasks. If you really cared so much about them, you'd take your own job a lot more seriously. It's any officer's DUTY," Kiel's eyes flashed when she said the word, "to discipline his troops. Life will be just that much harder on them when they assume their own duties in the fleet."

It sounded to Weston as if Kiel felt she had stumbled on the ultimate line to finally bring her around to the R.C.P.O.'s vision of the world. "Kind of like, spare the rod and spoil the child. Is that what you're getting at Kiel?" Weston rolled her eyes heavenward. "Has it ever occurred to you that those women are not children? No amount of discipline is going to make them do what they don't want to do when your back is turned. God, Kiel. I'm so sick of this argument." Weston's voice began to rise. "The truth, dear R.C.P.O., is that our power as company officers is totally illusory—"

"Yeah, but officers in the fleet—" Kiel interrupted.

"Oh, fuck the fleet, Kiel. They don't have any more power than we do. What do you think would happen if you gave an order to, say, march to the messhall, and the whole company decided they'd rather sleep in that morning? You'd march to the messhall by yourself, babe."

"That'd be mutiny. They'd all be court-martialed," Kiel exploded. "You could be written up just for suggesting it."

"So, I get thrown in jail. The whole company gets thrown in jail. And enlisted personnel the world over decide to sleep in one morning and they're all thrown in jail. Pretty soon, all you officers would be left standing around, picking your noses, issuing orders to each other."

Weston put her hand on Kiel's shoulder. "Look, Kiel, we all know the navy brass issues tons of orders that are shitwork. I figure our job as officers is to act as interpreters, wade through the crap and save us all a lot of time." Weston gently shook Kiel's shoulder. "Kiel, the whole thing is a big joke. Most of the women in this company laugh themselves to sleep every night thinking how dumb we are playing out this charade of being officers."

Before Weston could continue, Kiel wrenched herself free. "That's the stupidest thing I ever heard. If you think that, it's no wonder you're such a shitty officer. If we weren't so close to graduation, I'd replace you like that." Kiel snapped her fingers in Weston's face and then turned to march down the hallway.

"Fat chance. Who'd want the fucking job?" Weston bellowed after her.

Weston turned and charged into the recruit lounge, still smoldering from her encounter with Kiel. She located Jones and Harper and barged across the room in three great strides. "Well, are we going or not?"

Jones sputtered as she laughed. "Whew, I don't know. How many demerit points did you rack up for all that foul language, not to mention inciting a mutiny." She got up from the sofa and straightened her tie before offering Weston the crook of her arm. "Shall we go dance until the authorities apprehend us, Mr. Christian?"

Weston stared at Jones blankly, and then grimaced. "Oh funny, very funny. I actually feel more like the little boy who shouted the emperor has no clothes." Weston wrung her hands together. "On the other hand, it does tend to get one's blood up. I haven't felt this good all day."

They all laughed while Harper and Jones struggled into their overcoats. The three of them marched out of the lounge, unconsciously matching each other's stride. Only rigid military decorum kept them from actually linking arms as they made their way across the grinder to the gedunk. As it was, they walked so closely together that the skirts of their coats rustled companionably with each step they took.

With undiminished exuberance they crashed through the doors of the building where classes were usually held, quickly discarding their coats. They removed their soft caps and tucked them into the waistbands of their trousers at the small of their backs. Music blared from the decrepit jukebox, insisting they hurry lest they lose a single moment of the freedom it offered.

The three of them rushed forward, anticipation coloring their faces, and sailed into the cavernous lounge. The air was thick with cigarette smoke and the simultaneous conversations of a dozen groups of recruits.

They discovered Bates, Yont, and Taylor convened in a corner. A look of relief swept Yont's face as she turned her attention from the women she was with to the newcomers. Harper immediately disappeared, returning just as suddenly with two sodas in paper cups. She offered them silently to Weston and Jones and then quietly vanished to get one for herself.

Weston sipped her drink absently, only half-listening to the chatter. She slowly pivoted on one heel trying to encompass all that was happening in the room. The bass line in the current song pulsated throughout her body, seeming to threaten the very rhythm of her heart. She had a silly grin pasted on her face, and her eyes sparkled with pleasure at being so completely immersed in the loud music, the crowd milling about the room, and the cacophony of conversation. Her right foot unconsciously drummed along with each new song from the unsteady jukebox.

Harper reappeared holding her own soda and struggling to light a cigarette. Weston reached for, and captured, the paper cup before it splashed its contents down the front of Harper's trousers and shoes. Harper mouthed a thank you, then shrugged her shoulders at the futility of being heard. Weston grinned in reply. Jones wandered away to a knot of women surrounding the jukebox.

Harper leaned forward to reclaim her cup and yelled in Weston's ear, "What school have you applied for, after bootcamp?"

The assumption that most recruits entered bootcamp with was that a qualified woman applied to the school of her choice and got it. Especially now, when so many of the old rates, or jobs, that had been previously closed to women were opening up. What the friendly local recruiter failed to tell them, unless specifically asked, was just how many places each school allotted to women. There seemed to be a direct correlation between the prestige or price of the schooling, and a corresponding lack of openings for women recruits.

Finally, the most qualified recruit in the world who requested a rate with unlimited billets for women would still have to clear the last crucial hurdle—the prejudice of the personnelmen. Women personnelmen. Women who had entered the service when the only rates open to women had been those of yeoman, personnel, and radioman. Sometimes convincing these women that a woman could, and would, do a creditable job was harder than convincing a man. But that information was not in the glossy pamphlets handed out by the local recruiter either.

"What school have you applied for, after bootcamp?" Harper repeated above the din of voices.

Harper's warm breath tickled the nape of Weston's neck, and she felt goose bumps slide down the middle of her back. She hesitated, before leaning closer to Harper to answer, "Photo school."

A slow grin spread across Harper's face. "No kidding, me too." She stepped closer to yell above the noise. "Have you had much experience? I could show you some stuff." Just as suddenly, she moved away from Weston and made a great show of sipping her soda.

Weston searched the woman's face. Harper's eyes were unreadable as she stared into her cup, but a smile remained anchored near the corners of her mouth. Weston's mind raced, processing the sum of the quick smile, the glint in Harper's eye, the weight of her words. She knew innuendo when she heard it. She was not that dumb. A little voice inside of her was screaming, get me out of here. Just as insistently another little voice had surfaced, saying, well now, isn't that interesting. Jones saved her from further debate.

"I can't believe no one's dancing." She grabbed Weston's shoulders and moved them from side to side. "C'mon, let's shimmy, honey. Those girls would stand all day and talk." Jones jerked her thumb to indicate the recruits loitering around the jukebox.

"Oh, I don't know, Jones. I'm not feeling all that well," Weston stammered. "Besides, I'm an awful dancer."

Jones sighed in resignation. "O.K. I'll drag Harper out there then." She grabbed Harper's free hand and pantomimed the jitterbug. "Let's dance. C'mon, please?" Jones handed her soda to Weston. For a reply, Harper handed her empty cup to a woman nearby. Jones clutched Harper's hand and led her to a large clearing one side of the jukebox. Their circle of friends followed after them.

It was obvious in the way they moved together that Jones and Harper had danced together a lot. This familiarity was not lost on the many women who surrounded them in the crowded gedunk. Weston loved Jones' total abandon to the music. Harper's movements were more considered, studied, interwoven with what Jones did, and yet removed from her as well. Weston decided that they danced like good jazz sounded. As more women joined them on the dance floor, the crowd of watchers fell back to create additional room. Many faces bore sour traces of irritability, as if some persistent scourge had reappeared. The dominant expression on other womens' faces seemed to be envy. They looked as if they longed to dance but were afraid to take a step for fear of what it might imply.

Like a ship's mast in heavy seas, Yont's shoulders rolled and swayed to the music while her feet barely moved. Her thin frame seemed given to odd angles and shy, awkward movements. Sweat had captured the innumerable stray wisps of hair and molded them to her high forehead and long, elegant neck. She was completely lost in some deep communion within herself. Her partner, Bates, was like an engine on the loose. Head bowed in concentration, she moved her chunky arms and legs like pistons as she bulldozed circles around the stately Yont. Weston sipped her drink on the sidelines. It was enough just to be there. Her head pulsed with the music and her eyes roamed the dance floor, snapping mental photographs.

When the song ended, Harper and Jones strolled across the dance floor to join Weston. She handed Jones her soda. "You guys are just great together." Weston nodded toward the dance floor.

Jones laughed with delight. "We haven't even got going

yet." She lowered her voice in the sudden quiet between records. "Bev's family was always too broke to have a TV, so she used to come over to our house on Saturdays and watch "American Bandstand" with me and my sisters." Jones snorted, "Whatever Philly did in the morning, we all had down pat by Saturday night. Then we'd make up our own dances, too." Jones turned to Harper, "We could show Weston one, huh Bev?"

Weston immediately began to back away. "Now Jones, I told you I'm awful at this stuff."

"No, no. We'll pick an easy one. C'mon Bev, quick before the music starts again." Jones was grinning from ear to ear.

"Miss Jones, Miss Jones," the unmistakable voice of recruit Taylor boomed across the dance floor. Like the red sea, recruits parted and revealed the small woman hurrying toward the threesome. She held out her hand as she approached, "You simply must submit to the sublime experience of dancing with a sister from the City."

Jones turned raised eyebrows to Weston and Harper as if to say, I have no choice. She held out her hand to Taylor, who took it with an exaggerated swagger and led her to the center of the dance floor. Jones closed her eyes and waited for the music to envelop her. She picked up the beat and slid her shoulders and rolled her hips in silent testimony to her sheer joy in movement. Weston could easily imagine her, clad only in pajamas, leaping about the living room at home with her sisters.

Only inches away, Taylor's dancing transmitted something wholly different. The song was an innocuous adolescent wailing, and yet Taylor's body transcribed it into a seething cauldron of sensuality, full-blown, female sensuality. Taylor reveled in it, celebrating music and movement and herself as woman. Each woman's dance seemed to project a calculated extreme, and if they sometimes slipped into unconscious parody, that was all right too. Their eyes met during one such moment, and their laughter erupted spontaneously. They collapsed into each other's arms, laughing until they cried. Jones and Taylor and a small circle of dancers remained locked in orbit around the ancient jukebox until the gedunk closed just before the dinner hour.

16

"All right, who's missing?" Kiel's voice knifed through the silence in the hallway.

Anderson, the assistant R.C.P.O., scanned the marching formation of the company crammed into the hallway. "Looks like Weston." She paused, walking the length of the hallway. "And Taylor." Silence reigned again. This time it was an indictment.

Kiel looked pointedly at her watch. "Seventeen thirty hours. They know we muster for evening chow at exactly 1730 hours." She let her hand drop to her side. "We'll give them another sixty seconds, and then I'll have to award demerit points." Her feigned remorse fooled no one. No one moved. No one breathed.

At the head of the company, Yont finally broke the stillness. "Last time I saw them Weston was sitting on the spare bunk. Taylor had come to fetch her for chow."

Absolute quiet. Cramped, three abreast in the narrow hallway, in the stuffy barracks, sweat beaded on the upper lips of many recruits. It squeezed from the pores along their hairlines and ran in little rivulets between their breasts. The air was heavy with accumulated condensation from seventy-three pairs of lungs exhaling simultaneously.

Harper dismissed herself from the group. "I'll go see what's keeping them." She neither waited for permission nor a reply from the R.C.P.O. After a moment's hesitation, Kiel turned on her heel and followed Harper down the hall.

They arrived at Weston's cubicle in time to see Taylor ripping a blanket from one of the upper bunks. She noticed them, recognition flickering in her eyes, and then stooped and spread the blanket on the occupied bunk below. "Bout time one of you noticed we was missing." She tucked the blanket firmly around the inert form. Two visible cues informed them the occupant was Weston. Brown, poker-straight hair sprayed across the pillow, and a pair of wire glasses hung from the crossbar of the bunk bed.

"So, what's wrong with Wes?" Harper immediately stooped to peer into the shadow created by the upper bunk.

"She's sicker than a dog. Was shivering like a junkie when we got back from the gedunk. Thought dinner might make her feel better, but when she got up to go muster, phew!" Taylor shook her head. "Let's just say she'd still be kissing pavement if I hadn't been here to catch her."

Harper ran her hand over Weston's forehead. "Shit. She's hotter than Memphis." She turned to face Kiel. "We better call the officer on duty, maybe have her notify the base dispensary."

"Can't. The O.O.D. went to dinner five minutes ago. Just like we should have."

Taylor snorted. "Ain't that just what Weston was saying to me before she blacked out. I really should have done this earlier; the whole company will be late for dinner." Her voice had gone high and falsetto with her mimicry. Now it boomed across the bunk. "Just get the fuck out of here, Kiel. I'll stay with her until the O.O.D. gets back to the barracks." Taylor pulled the covers tighter around Weston's shoulders and then seated herself on a corner of the bunk with her back to the R.C.P.O., tacitly dismissing her.

Kiel's face flushed furiously as she sucked in her breath, lost for a reply. Harper's hand on her arm saved her. "She's right." Her tone was measured, calming. "There's not a lot we can do right now. We may as well get those women to dinner before the messhall closes. We'll notify the O.O.D. as soon as we can." Harper pushed the R.C.P.O. gently. "Go on, get them mustered."

Kiel let herself be soothed into letting the incident pass. She turned to leave the cubicle, then turned back suddenly. "And don't you dare do anything till I get back, seaman recruit Taylor." She pointed her finger like a gun. "That's an order."

"White bitch," Taylor cursed under her breath.

"I'll see what I can smuggle you to eat." Harper let her hand drop to Taylor's shoulder. "She's not really out cold, is she?" Harper's eyes sought the figure beneath the blankets and then searched Taylor's face.

"Naw. She never hit her head or nothing." Taylor patted Harper's hand. "Like you said, she's sure got one hell of a fever. You got your cigarettes on you? I left mine in my cube."

Harper reached down and extracted her cigarettes and lighter from the top of her socks. She dropped them into Taylor's lap and then turned to leave.

"And don't bring me nothing with tomatoes," Taylor called, as Harper left the cube.

"Gottcha. Hold the fort till we get back." She disappeared down the hallway.

Taylor leaned back against the wall, settled herself on the edge of the bunk, and then pulled a cigarette from the package. At the far end of the building she could hear the hollow explosion of the double doors slamming open and a muted version of Kiel's shouted orders drifting down deserted hallways. Then, the chuff, chuff, chuff of oxfords slapping the concrete floor. It started slowly, like a locomotive gathering speed as it leaves the station, grew more faint as the company exited the barracks, the heavy doors banged closed, aed slowly. Her free hand dropped to Weston's shoulder and stayed there.

Long minutes passed, another cigarette came and went, Taylor shifted carefully on her corner of the bunk. In spite of her caution, Weston's eyes opened, closed, and opened again. Directly in front of her was a lower bunk, olive-green, wool blanket stretched tightly across the mattress, gray metal bed frame, gray concrete floor, gray walls. Weston stared at them in momentary limbo and then her brain engaged.

She rolled over onto her back, throwing off one of the blankets in the process. "Jesus, it's hot." She wriggled her toes, felt an unfamiliar tightness around her waist, and reached one hand beneath the covers. "Hey, I've still got my uniform on." Weston turned a questioning face to Taylor.

Taylor snapped her fingers. "Damn, I knew there was something I forgot when I tucked you in earlier." She stubbed out her latest cigarette against the bed frame and let it drop to the floor. "You feel up to trying to change now?" She got up and moved toward Weston's locker and began removing bedclothes from the shelves.

Weston struggled to sit up on the bunk and felt a tidal wave of nausea surge from her gut upward. She clapped a hand to her mouth, squeezed her eyes shut, and waited. The moment passed.

When she opened her eyes again, Taylor was standing right in front of her. "You O.K.?"

Weston started with the buttons on her shirt, laboriously threading each through the corresponding buttonhole. It took both hands. Her eyes dropped to her shirt front, frowning with the effort it required to accomplish the task.

Taylor dropped Weston's nightgown on the bunk. "You keep working at getting your clothes changed. I'm gonna go down to the washroom and bring you some water. I think we should pump some aspirin in you before you conk out again." She bent down so that her eyes were level with Weston's. "O.K.?"

Weston had her shirt off by now and was fumbling with the buckle on her belt. Taylor picked up the nighty again and handed it back to Weston. "Don't worry about your pants. Get this on first, and I'll come back and help with the rest." Taylor rushed out of the cube as Weston began to ponder the difficulties of donning the nightgown. Somehow she managed it and then fell back on the bed exhausted. After a moment's rest she struggled out of her dungarees and left them in a heap at the foot of her bunk. It had been too much. She pulled the covers back over herself and rolled onto her side, snuggling into her pillow.

Taylor bustled back into the cubicle. "Hold your horses, sister. You ain't closing those eyes until you take these pills." She hurried over to the side of the bunk that Weston lay facing and stood there, tapping her foot. "C'mon. I can't take them for you." Taylor held out the glass of water.

Weston struggled to sit up, grunted once with the effort, and then closed her eyes against the dizziness. "It's not so bad if I keep my eyes shut. Just hand me the aspirin, then the water. O.K.?" Taylor did as requested, and Weston downed the pills along with the tiniest sip of water.

"Drink the whole glassful. You need lots of liquids with a fever that bad." Taylor stood and watched while Weston followed her orders. "And don't even think of throwing up." Taylor took the glass from Weston's shaking hand.

Weston's tone was softly belligerent as she settled back under the covers. "I haven't thrown up since fifth grade. And then it was only pretend so I could get out of Mrs. Hutchinson's math class." She turned on her side once again and opened her eyes. "It's lots better if I lie down and open my eyes."

Taylor returned to her corner of the bunk and seated herself once more. Weston watched her extract a cigarette from the package and light it carefully. Actually, she only heard the lighter click to life and the sharp intake of breath that indicated Taylor had lit it. Taylor inhaled, and the hand holding the glowing cigarette fell back and rested on her knee. Weston studied it a while.

"Have you always known you were Black, Taylor?" Weston asked softly. She felt the small woman beside her go rigid. She saw the hand disappear again, heard the slow intake of breath, a pause, and then her reply wreathed in smoke.

"In this society? A child knows in the womb she's Black."
Her hand came down and rested once again on her knee.

Weston closed her eyes again but continued talking. "In
some ways you're lucky things are that clear for you."

Taylor snorted her disbelief. "Only a little white girl could
ever make a statement like that."

"No, I'm serious." Weston groaned. "At least you grow up
never expecting life to be fair." She paused. "You don't get your
hopes up."

Taylor shook her head. "You're more full of shit than usual,
Weston." She hiked herself further up on the bed. "You really
think that's any way for a child to grow up?" Taylor blew smoke
out between pursed lips. "Besides, I've *never* quit expecting life
to be fair." She ground the butt out on the bed frame. "So, what's
happened to the company Pollyanna?"

There was a long silence. Weston opened one eye and appraised Taylor's face over her shoulder. "I guess I become a bit
of a cynic when I'm sick." She rolled over to look Taylor directly
in the eye. "But, O.K. Deep down I guess I still expect life to
be fair, too." She poked Taylor's thigh with her elbow. "Guess
that's why we get along, huh?"

Taylor scowled. "Well, you ain't exactly the pick of the lit-
ter. Especially at the moment." She withdrew another cigarette
from the package Harper had left her.

Weston mumbled as she snuggled into her pillow, "Sickly
cynical, cynically sick, sick, sick." She snored a ragged breath.

Taylor flicked the butane lighter and drew deeply on the
cigarette she held to her lips. Finished, she gazed down at the
woman next to her, listening to her breathe for a moment, and
then brushed the hair off her sweaty forehead. "Just what the
world needs, another cynic."

★　★　★

Throughout her dream, Weston could hear voices raised
in anger. It was as if there were a crowd gathered outside her
bedroom window, arguing.

"What do you mean, there's nothing we can do? So, the

officer on duty hasn't come back from dinner. Call Langhard. You have her number, don't you?"

"You said she was awake. She was up for a minute. It's not like she's going to die overnight."

"Jesus, Kiel. We don't know that. Anything can happen with a fever this bad. Call the base commander if you can't reach Langhard. At this point, who cares if the O.O.D. gets her ass in a sling as a result? You just can't take that kind of chance with Weston. Or with any of the women here."

"It's Saturday night. No one will be home anyway. Let's give the O.O.D. another hour or so."

"I can't believe this. You don't have to cover for them, damn it! They treat us like POWs for the last five weeks and then you side with them. Kiel, do something, cause I'm out of my league here."

"I will. I will do something. Lets just give the O.O.D. another hour. You keep on what you're doing. You're doing fine. Just fine, Taylor."

The voices evaporated and Weston was alone in her room at home. Her sisters were outside playing. She had decided to stay in and read. She heard the front door slam. A chair scudded across the living room floor. Whistling. Her dad was home. Drunk.

"Hello, I'm home. Any of my girls here?" Weston closed her book slowly and climbed off the bed. She opened her bedroom door and stood quietly listening. The whistling continued, loud and incoherent, from her parents' bedroom now. She could hear the clatter of closet doors, bureau drawers, other noise. What was he up to? This time.

She crossed the living room and stood in the doorway of their room, a frown creasing her brow as she watched her father sitting at her mother's small dressing table. He faced the mirror, leaning forward as she had often seen her mother do, and applied foundation to his cheeks and chin and nose. He caught sight of her in the mirror. A grin spread across her face.

"Hi, honey." His glee was infectious. Weston gritted her teeth against the smile that almost jumped to meet his. Invariably when he was drunk his pranks led to trouble. He waited a moment longer, then sighed and turned back to the mirror, reaching for the compact that her mother kept on the bureau. He added powder to his cheeks and nose with dainty strokes. Weston couldn't resist and crossed the room to stand behind him.

"What are you *doing,* daddy?"

He giggled. "Planning a surprise for mommy." He turned to face her. "How do I look?"

She frowned and studied her shoes. He looked ridiculous. There was a feeling she couldn't name. "It's not funny."

He searched her face. "Something's wrong." He turned to check his image in the mirror. "I know. It needs lipstick." He reached for the tube and created a red slash across his upper lip. He stuck out his lower lip and dabbed color on it.

"Daddy, that's mommy's favorite kind."

He winked. "Then she should like it even better on me." He rose from the bench and lumbered toward the closet. "Now, which dress do you think?" He glanced quickly at his watch. "Oops. We better hurry, the bus will be here any minute." He pulled a sleeveless summer dress from the hanger and yanked it roughly over his head. It fit him only because his hips were narrow and there were no sleeves to bind his shoulders. He stooped to roll up his work pants and shoved his feet into a pair of canvas mules. He tottered out of the bedroom and into the kitchen.

Weston had followed at a distance. He was busy shoving small drinking cups into the front of his dress. He modeled his new figure, hands on his hips provocatively. "Just like Jane Russell, huh?" He shuffled toward the front door. "C'mon. We want to beat the bus to the stop or it will ruin the surprise."

Once he left the house, neighborhood kids discovered him immediately. Like the pied piper they followed him down the narrow street. Weston had hung back, too interested in the outcome to stay home, but still struggling with her unnamed emotion. To the other kids this was an event, a happening, on a tediously dull street. But Weston couldn't forget the fact that this was her father, going to meet her mother, who would not find it funny.

She had spotted her mother on the bus about to get off.

Her father had arrived with his posse of laughing, squealing children just as the bus began to open its doors. Work-weary passengers flooded out of its portals. Her mother froze the moment she caught sight of the melee outside the bus. Her face said she only wanted to hide, to run as far away as possible. Seconds passed. Others pushed their way around her and continued to leave the bus. Weston's father kept up a running dialogue with the children outside, posing with one hand on his hip, fluffing his hair and applying more lipstick. Finally, when the bus driver could wait no longer, Weston's mother had squared her shoulders and exited the bus. The doors shushed behind her, and she was left alone with the havoc. She pushed through the throng, refusing to acknowledge it.

"Hey, good-looking. Buy a girl a drink?" He pouted his lips expressively.

Weston had watched as her mother had brushed roughly past him and marched toward the house. A sea of laughing, running children followed in her wake. She had wiped a tear brusquely off her cheek and kept walking.

"Jo-ie. Jo-ie, c'mon. Don't you have a sense of humor?" Her dad had hobbled after her.

Finally her mother exploded. "What was it exactly that you thought was so funny?" She kept walking, refusing to look at him. ". . .That you have ruined a perfectly good lipstick? Tore my dress? Things I've worked long and hard to be able to buy." Now it was her father's turn to be silent. "Or maybe the fact that you pulled such a stunt in front of the whole neighborhood." Her mother's voice had risen to a wail. "I'll never be able to get back on that bus again," she ended, sobbing.

"That you should be able. . .," the sobs began to trail off, "to humiliate me. It's just so unfair, Bill."

The rest of the long evening, before Weston and her sisters had been put to bed, was spent immersed in stony silence. Her father had cajoled; her mother had ignored him. Lying in bed, listening, Weston had finally heard her mother laugh. But it had sounded funny, alone in the dark, almost like her mother might cry again. Like there was a sob underneath the laughing trying to get out.

★　★　★

"So, how's the cynic this morning?" Taylor leaned over the bunk and her eyes searched Weston's face.

Weston moaned as she rolled over onto her back. "I feel like I've been hit by a truck. My head's killing me." She widened her eyes grotesquely and puffed out her cheeks in an imitation of someone throwing up.

Taylor held up her hand and laughed, "I get the message. Seriously though, when I'm over at the messhall I'll snitch you some dry toast. You should try and eat something today."

Weston struggled to a more upright position. "Where is everyone? The place is deserted."

"Gone. They've been tiptoeing around all morning, trying not to wake you." Taylor smiled. "Yont's off to church with some of the others. Bates is still in bed. Says she'd rather sleep than eat."

"Hi. Feeling any better?" Jones and Harper stopped just inside Weston's cubicle entrance.

Weston grimaced. "This is the worst better has ever felt. But yeah, I guess I'm gonna live."

The two women crossed to her bedside. Harper hesitated, then put the back of her hand to Weston's cheek. "Still pretty warm." She straightened, suddenly self-conscious. "We're just on our way to eat. Can we get you anything?"

Weston shifted her eyes from Harper to Taylor, then jerked her head slightly. "Ouch. My medical advisor here says that at some point in the day I'm going to develop an undeniable craving for dry toast." Weston shrugged and held up both hands.

"Dry toast it is then," Jones grinned. "You go back to sleep. Between the three of us we should be able to sneak you enough toast to last the day." The three recruits turned to leave as Weston snuggled back under the covers.

Jones stopped in the doorway. "Fortunately, it's the one thing they haven't figured out how to ruin." She raised her eyebrows comically. "Yet."

17

★ ★ ☆

"Company, forward HAR." Kiel set the phalanx of women into motion across the drillfield. Their shoes crunched on the gravel surface. It had stopped raining, but the nearby trees still held bobbins of water on the tips of the buds just beginning to swell. The air carried the smell of freshly turned sod, though there wasn't a farm field or garden for miles. The only explanation was spring. Weston watched incredulously as a fox scuttled across the bit of lawn before the supply building and disappeared around the corner. She felt like yelling *Stop* so the whole company could share this tiny bit of natural wonder streaking through the most unnatural of settings.

"Com-pan-ee, HALT." Kiel strode to the front of the column, passed them by three strides, executed a precise right-angled turn, stopped, stamped her feet, did another precise right-angled turn, and stood facing the first row of women.

"Today, ladies, we're going to be refitted for our dress blues. The tailors have done the bulk of the work, but now they want to reassess the alterations we were measured for in the first week of camp. This will be the final fitting before we receive our dress uniforms for our first leave from R.T.C.W." Kiel paused to look at her clipboard. "I don't have to remind you that this exercise does not involve the use of your mouths. Just answer whatever questions are put to you as efficiently as possible. All right, fall out and line up in alphabetical order."

While the rest of the women found their positions, the two women who regularly acted as doorholders for the company took their stations at either side of the entrance to the supply building. When all was ready, Kiel nodded regally to them and they swung the doors open. She was the first to enter and led the column of women, single file, to the rear of the building. Two fitting platforms waited in solitary splendor for the recruits. Four middle-aged women stood on either side of the small knee-high stations. Each wore a measuring tape draped around her neck, and a lapel of straight pins lined the dark blue smocks the navy issued them. Additionally, each wore a wristband pin cushion sporting more pins that bristled like pine cones where watches might have been.

The first recruit in line approached the far stage and mounted its steps. One seamstress accompanied her and began helping her into a navy serge jacket. She tugged and smoothed and patted the jacket into place while the other woman checked the length, the fall of the material from shoulder to waist. Chalk pencils sketched hasty details on cuffs and collars, then the jacket was removed. Next came the skirt. The recruit dropped her dungarees to pull on the skirt. The seamstresses made sure the material hung from the waistband in one smooth line to just below the knee, certainly no less, and if the recruit was a bit stocky, then perhaps a bit more. Off with the skirt. Next in line, please.

The line snaked along, one recruit after another. While the recruits that followed were being fitted, the first one off the platform was given moments to tidy her clothing and then led to another part of the building. There the supply clerk measured her head and located a hat box containing her new dress hat. Up until now the recruits had been wearing dungarees with white dress shirts, a uniform peculiar to bootcamp. Head covering had been their utility, or brevet, caps. These were made of thick, soft cloth and could be folded and shoved into a pocket when not being worn inside a building. The dress caps would still not be worn on a regular basis, until the recruits had passed to the next phase of their bootcamp experience and began wearing their dress uniforms daily. But acquiring the caps was a symbol, subtly suggesting that they had entered the homestretch. Graduation was certainly within their reach now.

"Jesus H. Christ, I got no more tits." Half of the company turned at the exclamation from the fitting platform. No one had any trouble recognizing the voice. Seaman recruit Bates stood holding the front of her blue serge jacket away from her chest. She grasped the material between forefinger and thumb as if it were something foul. The two seamstresses chuckled in response.

Bates caught Weston looking at her. "No kidding. Will you look at this, Wes?" She turned sideways so Weston could view the damage in profile. Bates picked at the cloth once again. "This was before," she declared dramatically, then let the jacket drop, "and this is after." The recruit audience awaiting their turns snickered. "God, I should sue the navy for defamation of my figure." The two tailors made a number of chalk marks on the outside of the jacket. Once Bates had removed it, the nearest woman slid the measuring tape from around her neck and slipped it around Bates' back, circling her breasts. With that finished, Bates stepped into her skirt. The same story—too big. More chalky shorthand and she was through. As Bates stepped off the platform she brushed by Weston and Taylor, standing near the end of the line.

"It's all that marching. My feet have grown a size and a half, and the rest of me has shrunk." She stopped momentarily to tuck her shirt into her trousers. "I just don't know what Ralph will say when he sees me again. He always said my tits were my second-best feature," Bates whispered to the two recruits in mock despair.

Taylor snorted in reply, "Well, don't you worry honey, there ain't a hope in hell of your best feature shrinking."

Bates grinned mischievously. "Why, whatever *do* you mean Miss Taylor? Ralph always said it was my eyes that were my *best* feature." Bates tossed her head and strode away. Taylor chuckled to herself as she edged her way back into the line-up. "God, she sure is a case, Weston." Taylor shook her head in disbelief. She caught Weston's eye. "So, you managed to keep breakfast down. Can you make it through the day?"

Still smiling, Weston nodded. "Yeah, actually the fresh air felt good." She patted Taylor's arm, "Thanks." She caught a glimpse of Kiel and the assistant R.C.P.O. striding across the room. "Oh no. Here comes trouble."

They both stopped just one pace short of Weston and Taylor. "How's it going back here?" Kiel demanded. She didn't wait for a reply. "The first half of the company's nearly finished. Anderson and I will take them back to the barracks to begin grounds detail. When the last half is through, you and Yont take them over to the classroom and commence grounds detail there. We'll muster at the barracks at 1150 hours and march to the mess-hall together." Kiel snapped the clip on her memo board to signify she was finished. It was an irritating habit that Taylor had been quick to mimic in the privacy of their washroom confessionals. Now, the shared intimacy of their laughter threatened to erupt any time they were together and witnessed Kiel's quirk of punctuation.

"Aye, aye," Weston responded, closing her eyes against the smile that tugged at her lips.

"By the way," Kiel started, then stopped and jerked her head toward the rear of the supply room. She strode several paces away from the women lined up behind Weston. Weston followed. Kiel dropped her voice. "I've been meaning to talk to you, but then, well you know, you got sick. Anyway, it's a little problem that I'd like you to handle." Kiel cleared her throat, then nodded toward Anderson, who had joined their circle but had not yet spoken. "It concerns your friend Bates." Kiel took a deep breath. "Andy here, and well, nearly all of the cubemates, have complained about Bates sort of talking in her sleep."

Quiet ensued. Anderson studied her oxfords. Weston looked from Kiel to Anderson and back again at Kiel. "Yeah. So?"

"Well, I thought you might talk to her about it," Kiel stammered.

Weston frowned, confused. "Me. Why me?"

"Because you're barracks M.A.A.," Kiel stormed, "and because I'm ordering you to. Why do you always have to make things so difficult?"

"Me make things difficult? The way I see it, someone in the cube should just go over the next time she starts babbling and shake the bunk till she wakes up." Weston was clearly exasperated. "Shit. Andy's making a mountain out of—"

Anderson exploded. "It's fine for you to say. But, she's not really sleeping, and the damned bunk shakes enough by itself." She turned to Kiel and fumed, "Oh, forget it, just forget it." Anderson turned on her heel and strode away without further explanation.

The R.C.P.O. cleared her throat again. "Anyway, Weston, I want you to talk to Bates. And that's an order." Snap went the clipboard.

"*Aye, aye.*" Weston opened her mouth to respond further, then closed it in resignation. She would talk to Bates. That was an order.

Kiel turned on her heel and followed Anderson. Weston stared after them momentarily and then returned to her place in the line-up. She could feel Taylor watching her, see her grinning face bobbing at her shoulder. Weston turned to her angrily, "So, what the hell was that all about? I know you heard every word."

Taylor's laugh was low and deep. It shook her whole body. Tears sat in her eyes as she finally slowed enough to gasp, hugging Weston around the waist. "Oh, honey. There are ten-year-olds in the City that ain't as dumb as you." A pained expression flashed across Weston's face. "No, now don't get me wrong," Taylor continued laughing, shaking her head in disbelief. "It's really kind of sweet."

18

Service Week, midpoint, half-way mark in bootcamp. The fifth week was spent suspended from daily classes. Recruits were farmed out to various areas in the recruit training command instead, to get a taste of what life in the fleet would be like. It was a week for following up on medical and dental work, personnel interviews, tying up loose ends. Plum assignments were at the drill hall or the R.T.C.W. staff offices. Weston couldn't figure this one out. Why would anyone want to work with C.C.s all day long, have to be on your guard, revved up and brown-nosing until quitting time every day? Nope, her assigned duty station suited her just fine.

She and a small number of recruits had been ordered to report to the M.A.A. of the R.T.C.W. staff barracks. The young women's reactions to their assignment varied pretty much according to their inherent feelings about R.T.C.W. and its staff. For some, it was akin to being asked to clean a movie star's home; for others, it was nearer to duty at the prison warden's house.

On that first morning of Service Week, Weston had marched her small contingent of recruits across the drillfield and down the concrete path that had been off limits to every other recruit on base. She had stopped them smartly in front of the low wood building and left them waiting at parade rest. She went inside to report their arrival to the M.A.A.

Her reflection in the polished floor tiles of the dimly lit hallway ushered her along to the far end of the barracks. It was quiet, quiet, quiet. In the same way her home had been quiet on those rainy spring days she had managed to convince her mother she was too sick to go to school. Once her sisters had all slammed out of the house on their way to classes, and her mother had left for work, peace settled over the whole house. It had always lifted Weston's spirits. On the days she really had been sick it had been all she could do to keep from throwing back the bedclothes and dancing around the room for the sheer joy of being alone.

Weston slowed her pace, reveling in the moment. She stopped, left foot planted firmly on the shiny, gleaming dance floor. Just one little pirouette. Weston looked up and down the hallway. She was totally alone; no one would ever know. She turned a small circle. Silence still. Throwing her arms wide, she turned once more, then again and again. She stopped at seven, a little dizzy.

In the nearest doorway, a woman leaned with her shoulder against the doorjamb. Her arms were folded over heavy breasts. She watched silently as Weston came to a halt, could see the fuzziness in the recruit's eyes, watched the expression on her face change as her head cleared and she became aware that she had been observed. The woman noted the blush that started below the recruit's starched chambray shirt collar, edged up her neck, and turned her cheeks scarlet. The young woman snapped to attention, scrunched her eyes closed briefly, and then opened them again. "Seaman recruit Weston, and five others, reporting for duty, ma'am." Silence.

The barracks M.A.A. looked directly into the younger woman's eyes. They were bright with fear, with embarrassment, and what else? Why? Why do this to these young women? she thought, as she had many times before. What do we gain by making them afraid of us, of the system? She held the recruit's eyes with her own, held them because she could not reach out to her in any other way. It had not been this way at all when she had joined, twenty years ago, during Korea. During that war, and the World War that preceded it, the navy had been glad to have its women recruits and treated them as something special. The older woman's mouth turned up slightly at the corners. If anything could be said of that navy, back then, it was that it tended to spoil its women recruits. She kept her eyes locked on Weston's until she saw the fear fade. Only embarrassment remained. The older woman smiled more broadly, and the young recruit ducked her head.

"Well, Weston, R. D.," the woman said, reading Weston's name tag. "Welcome aboard." She extended her hand, "My name's Hildebrandt. *Most* of the time you can call me Hilde." She winked at Weston. "I expect you'll know when the times are that you can't."

Weston took the outstretched hand in wonder. Touch— warm, deliberate touch. It was all she could do not to haul herself up the woman's arm, hand-over-hand, like a lifeline tossed into the sea. Hilde read the young woman's face, saw the disbelief, then the hope and the gratitude that came to take its place.

"C'mon. Let's put your girls to work, and then we'll have a cup of coffee. And for chrissakes, relax. It's not good for your spine to stand that straight all the time." Hilde grinned and stomped down the hallway to meet the other recruits. Weston followed discreetly behind her.

When Hilde reached the barracks door she stopped, giving herself time to survey the young women lined up outside. Finally, she smiled again and waved them inside. "C'mon. Get in here before it starts raining again." None of them moved, confusion registering on their faces. Hilde scowled. A protracted silence followed. Weston broke it by whispering to Hilde.

"They're not supposed to move until you bring them to attention. Then they can fall out." Weston hoped that she hadn't overstepped her bounds.

"Hell's bells. I keep forgetting that you're commando-trained. All right girls, ten-HUT and fall out." Hilde finished in a conversational tone. The new recruits still hung back, uncertain how to proceed in a situation that five weeks before had been the norm. Hilde waited patiently in the doorway. Once they were all inside the barracks, she strode off down the hall expecting them to follow.

At the first door Hilde stopped and motioned them inside the room. "As you can see, this here's the kitchen. The girls in this barracks keep it fairly tidy, but there are some things they just won't do." Hilde marched over to the stove and yanked open the oven door for the recruits to inspect. "Like clean the oven. That's where you girls come in. You two," Hilde jabbed her finger at the two recruits nearest her, "are assigned to the kitchen this morning." Hilde rattled off a list of tasks for the recruits to accomplish. "There'll be coffee at ten. We'll all meet in here. Then you break for lunch at—"she turned to Weston. "When's your appointment at the messhall?"

Weston thought hard before replying, "Twelve-fifteen," she started, and then her voice rose at the end of the sentence posing the question, "hundred hours, ma'am?" She hated the navy's system of telling time. Not because it wasn't logical. Quite the contrary, it made perfect sense. You never had to question if someone was referring to a.m. or p.m. But it was one more thing for the recruits to assimilate, one more thing to trip them up when speaking to staff and officers.

It was almost as if bootcamp was intentionally structured that way. So many new things were thrown at them at once. She rarely overcame the feeling of being off-balance. If one bit of information was easy to recall, something else would desert her completely at the very moment she needed it. And it seemed as if the officers would not, or could not, remind themselves that there was a time in their own pasts when they didn't know by rote all the rules and regs they pushed on the new recruits.

Hilde laughed. "This navy lingo's a pain in the ass, huh? Cleaning stuff is under the sink, you two. Now get down to it."

She moved out of the room and motioned for the others to follow. As she walked she pulled a large key ring from a loop on her belt and unlocked doors along the way.

"The other thing they won't do is windows. You three can start at this end of the hall and work back toward the kitchen. The stuff for this job is under the sink too. Now go on. With the three of you working, this side should be done by coffee time. We can finish the other side of the barracks before we break for lunch. O.K.?" She stopped at the door to her office and watched momentarily as the three recruits strode down the hall toward the kitchen. "C'mon in, you can help me with some filing while we talk." She smiled again at Weston and motioned her into the small office.

"Do you want some coffee?" Hilde pointed to a chair. "What do you take in it?" She handed Weston a mug and then settled herself in a large chair behind the desk. "Go on, sit down. You can't stand there all morning."

"How'd you wind up joining the navy? Look, don't think that it's all like bootcamp. There ain't no two ways about it, bootcamp is the pits. But once you get to a duty station, it's a lot like any other job." Her voice rolled on and on, washing over Weston, taking the stiffness out of her shoulders and letting her breathe free and deep for the first time in weeks. She was in no hurry to interrupt. She sipped her coffee and listened, nodding sometimes to encourage Hilde to continue.

"I've never understood why they start you girls out this way. It seems to me that if they were hoping to attract young girls to make the navy a career, they'd work harder at. . . ."

Weston felt tears forming in her eyes as she listened to the woman ramble. It was not so much what she said, although Hilde was obviously sympathetic to the plight of the recruits. Weston's reaction centered more around the simple hospitality of coffee and the opportunity to sit and talk as adults, as equals. Ever since she could remember, Weston had been encouraged to express opinions and make decisions at home. She had been allowed a great deal of autonomy, in large part because her mother was a single parent who worked to support the family. And she had been good at it, proud of the fact that she and her sisters had raised themselves.

The U.S. Navy had stolen that, and there was no indication that they would ever let her go back to making her own decisions or even appreciate her ability to do so. Then along came Hilde, and a light bulb went on in Weston's head. Weston swallowed a gulp of coffee hoping to wash away the lump that was clogging her throat. She couldn't stand Hilde being so nice, so matter of fact about it. Like it was everybody's due, that kind of respect. And it was. She wrenched her eyes away from Hilde's face and stared at a corner of the room where the ceiling met the wall. A tear slipped down Weston's cheek. To wipe it away would only call attention to its presence. Perhaps Hilde hadn't noticed.

Weston looked up at the ceiling, knowing that if she looked down now the tears would spill out of her eyes like a bowl of milk overturned on the breakfast table. She hadn't realized until this moment how much she both needed and wanted verification that reality was totally distorted at boot camp. And she hadn't realized how much it would hurt to have it verified. Like the hard part of being victimized is having to admit that it's happened, especially if it was someone you had trusted. And Weston had trusted the navy. Hilde's acknowledgment and concern were too much to bear. The tears ran down Weston's cheeks, and no amount of willing them to stop could halt them now.

Hilde sat a moment in silence watching Weston struggle for control of her emotions. Watched her lose the battle as the tears began. She put her cup down on the desk and rose quietly from her chair. "Take what time you need. I'll go check on the window washers." She let her hand rest on Weston's shoulder briefly before she left the room and closed the door.

Weston set her cup on the corner of the desk and gave herself over to the tears. She drew her knees to her chest, wrapped her arms around her legs, rocked herself, and cried. She shoved her glasses into the breast pocket of her shirt and rested her forehead on her knees. God, where did these tears come from? Her whole body ached with the effort of crying and still she could not stop.

Why had she joined the navy? Weston thought again of her mother and sisters, of friends at home whose lives had not changed. They all seemed perfectly happy with the way things were; she never had been. Why were they content planning lives as wives and mothers living within the world they had all shared? None of them had been cursed with the restlessness that afflicted Weston. She had thought the navy would be fun, exciting, a chance to do something different with all the energy she could barely contain. Instead it had stolen what little power she had.

Even as she mourned the past, however, Weston knew that there was no going back. There might never be an answer to *why* for her. But she would not let herself retreat, no matter how appealing the past might appear from the turmoil of the present. She sniffed back a deluge of tears and groped on Hilde's desk for a tissue. And the first step in forging ahead, she told herself, is to accurately assess the present with as little sentiment as possible. She wiped her eyes, blew her nose, and then sighed deeply. So, the navy wasn't going to live up to her expectations, not to mention the glossy brochures the recruiter had given her. She was stuck with it now, however. At least meeting Hilde had confirmed that she wasn't crazy: bootcamp was inhumane. It was the absolute pits, but it was a time-limited offer. Weston sniffed loudly. At this very moment she actually felt better than she had in weeks. She blew her nose one more time. It's a time-limited offer, and it's just five more weeks.

19

"REVEILLE." The word no longer held any terror for Weston. She had trained her internal alarm to awaken her half an hour before Kiel stormed through the barracks, clipboard in hand. Roll call was no longer the harried, frenzied affair of that first morning. Weston was usually dressed by the time it began. With roll finished, she secured her bunk and then found a quiet corner of the recruit lounge to retreat to while others flew around her trying to put their mornings together. Five minutes before departure, as other women were beginning to line up in the hallway, she began her rounds. Starting at one end of the barracks, she walked the passageways with Yont, making sure the area was secure before a single recruit was permitted to exit for breakfast. Once she and Yont pronounced the barracks satisfactory, the company could begin the day's activities with the march to the messhall.

After they signed out from the messhall, they marched directly back across the grinder for morning muster in the drillhall. How they marched depended, to a large extent, on how Taylor was feeling at the time. Under her cadence they strolled, they swaggered, or they paraded to and from their various destinations. Langhard may have picked Taylor for all the wrong reasons to be company cadence caller, but Taylor had repaid her a hundred times over once she discovered what a subtle and effective means it was of undermining Kiel's authority. Kiel could shout mark time, half time, or double time to her heart's content, but if Taylor's cadence was in three-quarter time, the company waltzed to its destination.

The C.A.s had made it clear that after the first two weeks of bootcamp and marching under "borrowed" cadence calls, the company caller must create her own for the remainder of camp. As angry as she was at the appointment, Taylor took on the project with a vengeance. At times she tried out her newest efforts on the group gathered in the washroom. At other times she waited to surprise them all, first trying a new call when the company was already in motion marching to yet another appointment. Weston got to the point where she was certain she could predict Taylor's frame of mind for the day by what she called for cadence in the morning.

The whole recruit command attended morning muster in the drillhall. R.C.P.O.s gave their reports to the C.C.s, the trooping of the colors was observed, and the plan of the day read aloud. During Service Week, individual recruit assignments were issued and appointments for interviews at personnel were broadcast. This extensive interview was a combination job screening, counseling session, and popularity contest. It was the hour when a recruit's future hung in the balance. If she had marginal scores on the proficiency test for the field of her choice, an outstanding interview could tip the balance in her favor. But it was rare that a recruit with a poor showing in a personnel interview would be accepted to any of the more difficult or prestigious schools, no matter what her test scores had been. Of course, this was not information available to the majority of recruits passing through the personnelmens' doors.

"Seaman recruit Weston, reporting as ordered, ma'am."

Weston stood rigidly at attention, not daring to move a muscle until directed to do so. She knew her uniform was perfect. Her oxfords gleamed in the tube lighting of the personnel office. Like most recruits she had a dress pair of oxfords that was kept at a spit-and-polish peak for inspections. They spent most of their life on the locker shelf, only seeing the light of day when it was of maximum benefit. Weston had brought along these shoes and changed just outside the doorway of the personnel office.

The yeoman writing at the reception desk finally looked up in annoyance, "At ease, Weston." Weston sighed audibly and smiled. She was ready for this—she was up, she was high. Her talk with Hildebrandt at the beginning of the week seemed to lift the weight of the world off her shoulders. The rest of that day felt like one long coffee break. She and Hilde had stopped occasionally to check on the other recruits, but mostly they had done paperwork in Hilde's office, and talked. Talked like real people. No ma'aming, no saluting or standing around at attention. It had been like a vacation, a slice of real life wedged into one of the longest running bad dreams she had experienced.

"Petty officer Parks will see you now," the yeoman motioned Weston through the nearest door.

Weston squared her shoulders deliberately, took a deep breath, and strode through the doorway. Relax, she told herself. Dad had said that in each job interview you should act as if you were meeting someone that you had heard a lot about and were excited to meet. He had been a world-beater when it came to getting jobs; he just couldn't hold on to them. She had lost count of how many times they had moved during her childhood because her dad was certain there was more to be squeezed from life in L.A. or San Francisco or Phoenix. It was Weston's mother who had finally made them settle in Phoenix. She simply refused to pack the family and follow him the last time he proposed a move. Smile, look them directly in the eye, and say to yourself, this person is going to give me exactly what I want. It had always seemed to work for him.

The petty officer at the desk looked up and motioned Weston to sit in the chair opposite her. Weston seated herself, folded her hands in her lap, and waited expectantly. Sit upright, look interested but not anxious, and don't fidget. Thanks, Dad. Weston let her eyes roam the room discreetly while the petty officer continued to scan the file on her desk.

"Well, recruit Weston, let's talk a little about your career." The petty officer pushed several pieces of paper aside and selected a particular form from the file. "I see from your educational profile that you've had a number of years of college. You were an excellent student, it says here. Why didn't you finish?"

Weston could tell by the way the woman accented the word *finish* that her incomplete college career was damning evidence that she was incapable of completing anything. Weston pondered the question. The fact was that she had never entered college with the thought in mind that she would come out the other end a finished product. Plenty of people along the way had tried to make her choose, had encouraged her to *be* something—anything. But at the end of two years, all she could say is what she didn't want to be. She didn't want to be in the small town in which she grew up any longer. She didn't want to *be* in the same way that others around her were choosing to be mothers, teachers, secretaries. She had discovered photography in her third year and thought she might become an artist. There was no money to find out, however, and she was tired of being a poor student.

"I'll be frank with you," Weston leaned forward, taking the woman into her confidence, "I discovered photography in college. My instructor felt that I had talent and should go to one of the good photographic schools, or at least a college with an excellent fine arts program. I simply couldn't afford the better schools, and it would have taken years to put together a portfolio good enough to apply for a scholarship. The navy seemed a likely alternative. I hear the training at its photographic school is pretty extensive."

Weston sat back and slowly exhaled. She raised her eyebrows, suggesting the question, "What was I supposed to do?" She hoped that the woman would be somehow flattered to think the navy photographic training might be equated with the better colleges. Dad had always said, tell them what they want to hear. Weston really had no idea how the two compared, so it was a bit of a gamble bringing it up. But then, she was sure the woman seated across from her would have no idea either.

The woman smiled at Weston for the first time. "Well, you know the costs of the navy photographic school aren't cheap. We like to make sure that the recruit we send from R.T.C.W. will do well and has a sincere interest in photography. Some young women are only interested in a duty station in Florida."

Weston looked at the woman blankly.

"Usually there's a waiting period of several months before you can enter a new class. Then the school is several months long as well. All told, you can look at being stationed in Florida for as long as six months," the woman droned on.

Slowly, a sense of what the woman was saying crept into Weston's consciousness. Warmth, palm trees, white sandy beaches, warmth. Months of it. Her look of disbelief was genuine. She might get an appointment to a duty station in Florida, someone to pay for her photography lessons, and if Harper went too, she would actually know someone there. Life could not be that incredible.

Driving any note of hope from her voice and pitching it to match the look of surprise she knew was on her face, Weston replied, "You're kidding! You mean some people actually choose their career based on a school's location?" The expression on the petty officer's face told Weston that her voice had been the perfect blend of surprise and outrage.

The woman leaned forward across the desk and dropped her voice. "Oh, it's far worse than that. Why, some of the more expensive schools in Barcelona, or the one in Athens, are constantly turning down applicants who aren't even qualified. It seems they apply simply because it looks like a chance to vacation in an exotic place at U.S. Navy expense." Her pursed lips as she leaned back in her chair gave final condemnation to the scoundrels.

Weston had a fleeting moment of indecision. Perhaps she had been too hasty; maybe she didn't really want to be a photographer. The thought of Florida was nice, but Barcelona. . . . She wondered briefly how a recruit found out what navy schools were located in neat places like Athens, or Cairo. She had always wanted to go there.

"Yes, it could easily sour you on the subject of human nature. Sometimes I feel that every young girl who comes through that door is out to rip off the U.S. Navy anyway she can." The woman sighed heavily.

Weston made consoling noises from her side of the desk. She wondered if it had occurred to the petty officer that if the navy were as concerned about being ripped off as she was, they'd put their schools at the North Pole. Then, for sure, the only applicants would be those who really wanted the schooling. She thought it in her best interests not to share this thought with the woman from personnel.

"Of course, my biggest concern is that the navy recoup the cost of training you as a photographer. We know from your academic record that you should be able to do the theory, and the practical assignments shouldn't be any more difficult than your college work."

Weston forced her mind back into the present, nodding her head in assent.

"Well, I know this isn't very delicate, but are you going to meet some strapping fellow and get yourself knocked up in that famous Florida moonlight and have to quit the service?" Petty officer Park pushed her chair away from the desk. Her eyes bored into Weston's.

Weston's mind registered shock. She struggled to keep her face impassive. She was shocked on so many levels she couldn't catalog them all. The woman's choice of phrases was crude, insensitive—just like a man's, Weston thought. She was appalled that the woman seemed to feel it was her right, her duty, to delve into Weston's private life. How could another woman be so callous about such an invasion of privacy? Weston's mind churned, processing her anger.

For the first time Weston stopped and made herself really look at petty officer Park. Her black hair was close-cropped, brushed back off her face. She wore a silver identification bracelet on one wrist. There was a square, blockish ring on the baby finger of her left hand. Weston belatedly looked into the deep-set eyes across from her. She had met this woman a million times on basketball courts in high school and baseball diamonds during the summer softball season. There was no shock of recognition in the eyes of petty officer Park because she had assumed she knew everything there was to know about seaman recruit Weston the minute she walked in the office door. Now she only awaited confirmation.

Weston knew she could rant and rave about the unfairness of the question. She deserved to get into photography school on the basis of her own merit. She was qualified; she could do the work. She wanted to shout, *Fuck you, petty officer Park.* Instead, she held the woman's gaze, pushed all the issues of fairness or favoritism aside, and answered, "That won't happen."

Three words was all it took. By the expression on Park's face, Weston knew that the position was as assured as petty officer Park could make it. She should feel elation, but all there was drifting down from the hypercenter of her brain was disappointment. It fell slowly, gently, as Park droned on explaining the details of the navy's new rating system. Park had relaxed, her manner was amicable, as if talking to a peer. Weston, on the other hand, felt deep waves of anger and frustration rolling in. She was disappointed at herself for not being more vocal. The anger was more generalized. Some was directed toward the personnel officer for failing to ignore her own built-in biases. What if she had wanted to marry and have children? That was certainly no reason to deny her a job. Weston could feel her anger at the system growing, a system that said repeatedly, *We'll use you because we have to. But the very fact that you are a woman makes everything you do suspect.* And petty officer Parks obviously agreed.

20

Saturday morning of Service Week, their first "shore leave," their first opportunity to leave R.T.C.W. in five weeks of training. Women spilled from their beds and lined up, as usual, for morning roll. All around her, on both sides of the corridor, Weston could feel the same insolence she felt in herself. She hoped Kiel was astute enough to pick up on it but not react. In the oral tradition, handed down from company to company, she had never heard of a company not being allowed to go on liberty. But that didn't mean it couldn't happen. Weston had a sinking feeling this was just the kind of first this group of women would garner. She found herself praying to Kiel as she passed. Don't push them, just don't push them this morning.

Kiel was such a powder keg herself that Weston was hesitant about approaching her with her feelings. Instead she paced the barracks corridor, encouraging women to be prompt in dressing and to remember to secure their areas. She passed Taylor's cube and stuck her head around the open locker door. Taylor held a mirror in one hand while she poked and prodded her hair with the other.

"Oh, honey, there ain't a blessed thing you could do to make yourself more beautiful this morning." Weston grinned and stood surveying Taylor with her hands on her hips.

Taylor beamed into the mirror at Weston's reflection hovering over her shoulder. "Ain't that just the truth?" She shelved the mirror and turned to face Weston.

"So, how do I look?" Taylor ran her hands down the front of her jacket to smooth any wrinkles.

Weston looked her over critically for a moment. She knew she should not let the smile on her face say too much and clung tenaciously to the words that almost escaped, words that would only embarrass them both. With immense effort she did not say *I love you,* did not take the small woman and dance her around the room, did not grab her and pound her on the back and shout, *We have made it. Nothing, ever again, could be this bad, and we have survived it together.*

Instead Weston reined in her smile and joked, "Shit, you must have on black panties, cause if they were white those shoes are so shiny I'd for sure see their reflection."

"Hoo-ee, show's you what you know." Taylor grabbed Weston and spun her around. "You think if I'm going to the big city for the first time in five weeks I'd even bother wearing panties?" Taylor laughed uproariously and slammed her locker door. She grabbed her coat in one hand and Weston's arm with the other. "Let's go have some chow and then git on that bus." She guided her along the hallway to the lounge. "What's the first thing you're gonna do in Lancaster?"

"I'm going to find me a restaurant and sit down and order coffee. Weston paused for effect. "Then I'm just going to sit there and enjoy every step that waitress takes while she gets it and brings it to me."

"That's it?"

"Well, no. Once I finish drinking that cup, I'm going to give her a great big tip, then find me another restaurant and order me another cup of coffee. I intend to spend the whole day in coffee shops having someone wait on me and paying them exorbitantly for their services." Weston sighed. "I might read the paper some, too."

Taylor howled, her laughter echoed up and down the hallways. She doubled over and pounded her thigh. "You do beat all. They kidnap us, then keep us locked up for five weeks, and it turns out the thing you miss most is a second cup of coffee in the morning." Taylor sobered immediately when she noticed Weston's scowl. She raised her hands in surrender and shrugged, "Different strokes," but a smile still curled the corners of her mouth.

For once the whole company was finished eating and waiting for Kiel to ask permission to leave before their allotted time was over. She signed them out as soon as protocol would allow, and they began the march back toward the barracks. Across the grinder and past the drillhall, Taylor's cadence had them swinging in a rhythm that was beautiful to behold. From the corner of her eye, Weston spotted a rag-tag bunch of women marching on the grinder parallel to them. Baby boots with their C.A.s in tow. They slowed their pace perceptibly as Weston's company approached. At that moment, Taylor ended the cadence she was calling and bellowed a simple LEFT, pause, LEFT, pause. This always signaled the beginning of a new call.

Weston's eyes registered a flash of recognition as their company swaggered by the baby boots. C.A. Hernandez had halted the young women so they could watch the senior company pass. How to say hi, we're doing very well, thank you? But, most of all, how to say thank you? Weston knew they must look great. It certainly felt wonderful to see Hernandez again, even briefly. Shit, Weston thought, Taylor must have seen her too.

Suddenly, Taylor's voice shifted and then rang out, "Hip-ho, ladie-O."

There was the merest hesitation. Then Weston's voice bellowed in reply, and the others followed suit, "Hip-ho, ladie-I."

"Hip-ho, hop-ho, wring out your mop-O. Your LEFT, your right, your left. Sound off."

Weston could see the babies stopped, watching their passage across the grinder. She caught a glimpse of Hernandez shaking her head and smiling. And then, as if it were in slow motion, Weston saw Hernandez raise her hand and salute them, briefly, crisply. In a moment they were by them and headed for the bus. For the second time that day, Weston could have hugged seaman recruit Taylor.

★ ★ ★

It was not a sunny day, their first leave from R.T.C.W., but it was not raining. The old bus discharged its cargo, and the young women clustered near it, suddenly grown shy of facing the world in all their new regalia.

Removed from the context of R.T.C.W., the dress caps and navy serge skirts and jackets they had worked so hard to attain now seemed more than a little matronly. Slowly, small groups of women broke off from the larger group and began a hesitant promenade down the main street of Lancaster. They checked their watches dutifully and suddenly realized they had hours to fill until their mustering time that evening, and no idea how to fill them. Ten p.m. at the Lancaster U.S.O. was a long ways away.

21

★ ★ ★

Pumps. Black pumps. Weston strolled along the sidewalk looking in the shop windows. Supposedly the whole purpose for this little adventure, she told herself, was for the women recruits to have an opportunity to complete their dress uniform by purchasing black pumps. She caught a reflection of herself in a shop window. Hat at right angles to her eyebrows. Lipstick neatly applied. She hated the taste and tried not to lick her lips any more than was necessary. But the perfumey taste of the stuff was pervasive. Why would the navy insist that lipstick be part of their uniform? Men didn't have to wear it.

She turned and continued walking. Weston hitched the newspaper she carried higher under her arm and readjusted her purse strap on her shoulder. She noticed with distaste that news-print had left a dark smudge on the tips of her white gloves. Shit. Lucky she had thought to bring her other pair with her. Still, she would have to bleach these as soon as she got back to base to have a clean pair ready for inspection on Monday.

Parading around town in her new dress uniform was fine in theory. What Weston had quickly discovered, however, was that it was a lot like the fancy Easter outfits she had gotten as a child. They looked great for the annual Easter family photo and were fine as long as she only sat in a church pew. But they were absolutely hopeless if you tried to actually live in them. She wished wholeheartedly that she was back on base in her dungaree uniform. She was tired of being gawked at by rumpled young men whose hair was many times longer than her own and who seemed to view her as a museum piece set loose on the streets. Coffee gurgled in her stomach with every step she took.

Weston sidled past the movie theater, checked her watch, and then looked longingly through the glass double doors. The lobby lights were on now, and the popcorn machine glowed on the counter top, filling the air with its aroma. An elderly man was pushing a vacuum back and forth across the carpeted lobby. He looked up briefly. Weston waved. He flicked the switch on the machine, and the heavy hum gradually subsided. Then, his voice gruff, he cracked the door and said, "We don't open for another twenty minutes."

Weston's expectant smile faded, and she looked down at her feet. "I know." She looked back into his face hopefully. "Could I just come in and read my paper until the movie starts?" He hesitated. "Please."

"O.K., O.K. But sit around the corner where no one can see you, or I'll have every Tom, Dick, and Harry wanting in early too." He looked furtively up and down the sidewalk, making sure the coast was clear before he opened the door just wide enough for Weston to enter. He motioned for her to sit on the bench nearest the women's washroom.

Weston crossed the lobby and sank onto the bench gratefully. Off came the hat and the gloves. She dropped her purse on the floor next to the bench and bent down to loosen the laces on her shoes. With one deft hand she managed to unbutton her serge jacket while pulling at the toe of her nylon stocking with the other. The seam that ran across her big toe had rubbed a small blister from being on her feet most of the day. She had foolishly worn her dress oxfords; they weren't anywhere near as comfortable as her other pair. Too little use. She sat and breathed deeply the theater smells of popcorn and stale cigarette smoke. If she closed her eyes for just a moment, she could almost see the old movie house in Phoenix where she and her sisters had gone nearly every Saturday of their lives. You could get in for twenty-five cents and a pop bottle top if you were under twelve—a whole day of second-run movies and cartoons. She smiled to herself. Here it was Saturday afternoon and she was once again killing time at the movies. Weston laughed outright. It was supposed to be so different being an adult.

She roused herself once she began to hear voices in the lobby entrance. Weston wearily pulled herself back together and started toward the box office. The old man was encased in glass, selling tickets through the wicket. He spotted Weston approaching from across the lobby and waved her away. He jerked his head toward the theater seats and winked. She flashed him a peace sign and then hurried to find herself a seat. Half-way down, center section, right on the aisle—the perfect seat was waiting, and Weston settled into it. She dropped her head back on the seat rest and closed her eyes until the house lights dimmed.

★　★　★

Weston stepped through the open door of the U.S.O. It hadn't been far from the movie house and was easy enough to find. She was a few minutes late and wasn't sure what to expect. She had visions of Kiel lining them all up on the dance floor and doing an immediate roll call. A burly sailor in dress-blue uniform blocked the second doorway. Weston felt his eyes pass over her from head to foot before he deigned to move aside. A quick look of annoyance flickered across Weston's face.

"Just checking. There's no civilians allowed, unless accompanied by a sailor."

"Don't mention it. I noticed a lot of civilian women are wearing outfits like this these days." Weston scowled at him as she passed. She passed through the second door and stopped immediately to survey the room. On the far side, red, white, and blue streamers and bunting adorned the corner where a punch bowl sat atop a card table surrounded by a variety of glasses. A number of formica-topped tables, remnants from someone's kitchen, and an array of chairs were scattered about as well. A mirror globe hung from the ceiling over the dimly lit dance floor and spun on its axis, casting fragments of rainbows among the five or six couples attempting to dance. Weston caught the movement of a hand waving in her direction over to the right of the dance floor. She instantly recognized Jones, Harper, and Taylor sitting with two other recruits she didn't know.

"Great, I was hoping you guys would already be here." Weston pulled up another chair and sat down next to Taylor. "What you been up to? Where's Yont? Has Kiel jumped ship?"

"Little Kiel Hitler? We should be so lucky." Taylor leaned toward Weston and waved her hand to indicate the two unknown recruits. "Smith and Wesson." She leaned her arm along the back of Weston's chair. "No, you're Wesson. This here's Smith and . . . ," she giggled. "I don't know, what is your name?"

Weston drew back from Taylor's face so close to hers. "Phew, what have you been drinking?" She looked anxiously in the recruit's glazed eyes. "No, forget that. How much have you been drinking?" Weston turned to Jones and Harper, "Can she walk?"

Jones laughed, "Well, she gets by, although she has developed a distinct list to starboard. I've been encouraging her to drink coffee for the last hour. Hasn't had much effect."

"Where's Yont?" Weston turned from scrutinizing Taylor's face to surveying the room.

Harper smiled at her concern. "She's safe enough. She's dancing with a fellow she met this afternoon at the hardware store."

Weston checked the dance floor absently, then frowned at Harper. "The hardware store?"

Taylor guffawed, "Hoo, don't ask."

Harper continued patiently. "Yeah, she spent most of the afternoon there looking through their seed catalogues and just browsing. Said it reminded her of home." All the faces around the table wore indulgent smiles. Weston smiled in response.

"How bout you. What'd you do all day?" Harper's voice sounded tired to Weston. She looked again at their faces and noticed they all wore the same weary mask.

"Drank coffee, read the paper, and watched a couple of movies." Weston sighed. "I don't know about you guys, but I was ready to go home four hours ago." She fell back in her chair.

"No kidding. Me too," echoed around the table.

"Who's idea was it to take in this dance?"

"Oh, the command always plans it that way," the unnamed recruit spoke for the first time, "to coincide with the men's liberty. That way the sailors don't have to worry about dates their first night ashore."

Five pairs of eyes turned to confront her. "You're kidding?" Jones glared.

The woman sighed. "Everyone knows that. The base commanders encourage their men to go to the U.S.O. for the evening for some good, clean fun. Us."

Taylor leaned over Weston again. "I can see why they keep women recruits so isolated. Talking to other women in the navy only confirms my worst suspicions about old Uncle Sam." She crossed her arms over her chest and nodded toward the woman. "Weston, this is seaman Rittel. Graduated top of her class three weeks ago."

Rittel smiled, "So you had your personnel interview last week. All of you? What school? How'd you do?"

Weston caught Harper's gaze quickly, then answered Rittel. "Photo. I think I did O.K."

"Oh, go on. Tell em what you told me," Taylor elbowed Weston. "She said she figures she's got it aced. She did everything but sit on the woman's lap and tweek her tits." Taylor pounded the table with her hand as the word *tits* left her mouth. "And I said, whatever it takes honey, cause the navy isn't gonna give you nothing for free."

Weston groaned. "I didn't exactly use those words."

They all laughed at Weston's expense. She felt her face color under their scrutiny. "Taylor's right, though," Rittel interrupted, "you better stand on your head if you have to. Especially for something like photo school." She paused and then continued. "I heard they only ever pick one woman from each class to attend. If you don't do something to stick out, you haven't got a hope in hell of being chosen." The table grew suddenly silent.

Weston could not meet Harper's eyes. She felt them on her, begging her to look up. She knew what they would say. *It's all right, you didn't know. If only one person can be chosen, I hope it's you.* That was what Weston couldn't face, knowing she couldn't say the same. Even if she had known, she couldn't swear she wouldn't have done everything possible, have stood on her head if that's what it took, to make it into photo school. And because she couldn't swear it would have been different, in her heart of hearts, she hated herself for doing what it took to get what she wanted. It never occurred to her to hate a system that forced women to choose constantly between loyalty to it, to themselves, and to other women.

"Sst," Taylor hiccuped in her ear, "don't look now, but I think a certain woman recruit is dancing in her sleep."

Weston's head jerked toward the dance floor, where all the couples were engaged in trying to sort out a method of movement that combined the maximum amount of physical stimulation with the least amount of motion. Something erotic that could still be camouflaged as dancing to the slow music humming from the speakers.

"We're fine for now, but as soon as a jitterbug comes on," Taylor wheezed, "her partner may recognize that she done left the party, so to speak."

"Shit, no kidding," Weston whispered in reply. "What'll we do?"

"Whatever it is, it better be soon." Taylor sat bolt upright. "Sounds like this is the tail end of this song." She grabbed Weston's hand and pulled her to her feet. "Quick. Go cut in."

"What?"

Taylor grabbed Harper's shoulder and pushed her out of her chair. "You too," she shoved. "Doesn't make any difference what you say to em. But you better do it now."

Strains of music from the next song were beginning to drift

from the speakers. Weston hurried toward the couple on the dance floor. Harper wasn't far behind her.

Weston tapped the young sailor with Yont on the shoulder. As courtesy dictated, he immediately backed away from his partner to surrender her to a new swain. He turned to speak to the interloper and then froze on the spot.

Weston blushed furiously but took Yont's hand and circled her waist with her arm. "This song's kind of special," she stammered. "We always dance to it, you know, when they play it," she was running out of breath, "back on base. Well, it's like it's our song." She whirled Yont away before the fellow could reply.

Harper never gave him time to say a thing. "I've had my eye on you all night, guy." She grabbed his hand. "Now that you're free, let's dance." She pulled him around so that he could no longer see Weston or Yont. "You come here often, or is this just my lucky night?" Harper tilted her head and smiled up into his eyes.

Weston did a few quick turns with Yont and then steered her toward the table where the others waited anxiously. Taylor pulled out a chair and Weston pushed the somnambulant Yont down into it. Rittel was looking on with more than a passing interest. A question was framed in her eyes, and her mouth formed a tight thin line.

"Look, I said you can't bring this guy in here," the sailor from the entryway bellowed into the room. "Sailors and waves only." All heads turned to catch the altercation starting across the room.

"Fuck you, asshole. You said sailors and their dates." Seaman recruit Bates turned on him accusingly, never letting go of the hand she held. "Well, I'm a sailor and this is my date." She jerked her head to indicate the man whose hand she held. His blond hair flowed down across his shoulders, and his eyes were glazed in what could have been permanent amazement.

"Oh, far out. I never thought I'd see the inside of the U.S.O. It looks kind of like the old high school dances, hey." He turned to see if recruit Bates shared his amazement.

The doorman wouldn't let up. "Look it, sister, I may let him in since the dance is almost over. But whatever you got in that bag has got to go." He made to grab at the brown paper bag that Bates held in her other hand.

She twirled away with her partner, her laughter catching in the corners of the old hall. She tossed the doorman the bag that was obviously wrapped tightly around a bottle. "If you're collecting empties, it's yours baby." Bates turned her back on the doorman, ending further discussion. She and the civilian took their time parading to the table where Taylor and the others waited. The lights on the dance floor flickered, signaling the last dance. Harper excused herself to return to the table and her friends, leaving the young sailor alone under the mirrored globe, a perplexed look on his face.

"Well, all the chickens have come home to roost and none too soon, I say." Taylor grinned and motioned toward the doorway. Kiel and the assistant R.C.P.O. were striding through the door. "Seig Kiel," Taylor laughed harshly, and her rigid arm began to rise in mock salute.

Weston grabbed it quickly, "Cut it out and help me with Yont." She pushed Taylor toward the tall recruit's chair. "She's groggy, but I think she's awake now."

"I never *was* asleep, I told you," Yont insisted, as Taylor and Weston helped her rise and start for the door.

"Roll call before we board the bus. FIVE minutes, ladies," Kiel's voice echoed in the rapidly emptying hall.

Once outside the building the recruits automatically lined up, single file, in alphabetical order facing the bus. The R.C.P.O. strolled the formation checking off names on her clipboard. Once each woman's name was called, she was then permitted to board the bus.

"Anderson, Arrons," Kiel read out, eyes flicking from her clipboard to the respective recruit's face. "Arthurs, Bates, Bellows. BATES."

Seaman recruit Bates was locked in a crippling embrace with the young man with the flowing hair. He pulled away sheepishly and pushed her toward the bus. She boarded without a backward glance toward the furious R.C.P.O. Once aboard, Bates hurried to a window seat and immediately lowered the bus window.

"Yoo-hoo, sweetie." She waved what appeared to be a white hanky from the window. The young man approached, and she tossed the hanky his way. It fell to the ground before he could catch it, at Weston's feet. She stooped quickly and retrieved it for him. As she straightened to hand him the hanky, she recognized the gift was not a hanky at all. Seaman recruit Bates had tossed the young man her panties.

22

☆ ☆ ☆

Every woman in the company was grumpy the next morning. They were all grateful for the no-talking rule at breakfast. They suffered the kind of emotional hangover that hits people after a big event like Christmas or New Year's. You invest enormous time and energy before the holiday, anticipating what will happen. The first letdown is that the actuality rarely lives up to the fantasy you've been building in your head. The biggest letdown comes the day after when you go back to your ordinary life without even anticipation to flavor it. If yesterday's vacation in Lancaster had been to celebrate the end of five weeks hard, dreary slog through the first half of bootcamp, today marked the beginning of five weeks of more of the same. Weston was not happy.

They all clumped back to the barracks, the pools of rain water on the grinder slopping up the cuffs of their dungarees. Shit, Kiel couldn't even lead them around the worst of them, Weston thought to herself. She should consider doing some laundry when they got back to the barracks. It seemed too much effort, though, and your clothes just got dirty again anyway. If she could do anything she wanted, how would she spend the day? Weston loved playing this game. She could hear Taylor calling cadence, a dispirited "Left, left, left." She'd find a really good book. That's what she should have bought in Lancaster yesterday. She was sick, sick, sick of reading navy history, memorizing military insignia and the rules and regs. She'd find a good book and crawl back into bed and spend the rest of the day reading and napping. And at dinnertime Mom would call and say, "Come on down to dinner now. It's chicken and dumplings, your favorite."

Weston suddenly laughed at herself. Well, honey, nice dream. What are you really going to do? They entered the barracks and Weston went straight to her cube and opened her locker. She removed her shoes and wet socks, took two clean pairs from the shelf and put them on. She dug out her slippers and put them on over the socks. Notebook in hand, she strode down the passageway toward the fire escape. The exit door beckoned her. She looked around briefly, opened the door, and then shut it firmly behind her. She could still hear locker doors slamming, chairs scraping as they were moved, and bits and pieces of conversation. But they were gloriously muffled, more dreamlike than real. She pulled her coat tightly about her and lowered herself to the floor in the corner of the stairwell. She pulled her knees up to her chest and turned to face the wall. For sure she'd have a crick in her neck when she woke up, but God, this was great. Quiet and alone.

★　★　★

Weston felt a persistent prod against her foot. If she ignored it, maybe it would go away. Again. She moaned aloud. Ugh, how long had she been curled up like this on the cement? Probably not that long. It had seemed to take forever to get to sleep. Aah, where was she? Bootcamp, where else. She opened one eye and just as she did Yont prodded her once again with the toe of her oxford.

"I've been looking all over for you." She made no move to sit down. "I want to talk to you."

Weston took warning from Yont's tone of voice, her failure to join her on the stairwell floor. "This may not be a good time, I'm just waking up. And," Weston hesitated, "you sound a little grumpy." She sat upright and was jolted by an incredible spasm in her neck. Weston moaned again. "Can we talk later?"

"*No.* This can't wait." Yont placed her hands on her hips and glared down at Weston. "What was the big idea cutting in on the dance floor yesterday? Was that your idea of a joke?"

Weston looked up at Yont's face and immediately regretted it. Pain shot across her shoulder. "What? Is this what you woke me up for?" She could feel herself starting to burn inside, anger boiling up from the pit of her stomach. "Well, it wasn't my idea. But it just may have saved your precious military career." She said with more irritation than she meant to let slip, "I told you. You had fallen asleep on your feet."

Weston struggled to her feet. Reaching out with one hand to use the wall for support, she slowly straightened up. "It wouldn't have taken that yokel you were dancing with more than twenty seconds to figure that out once the new song started. Harper and I did what we thought was necessary." She spread her hands out before her in a gesture of helplessness. "I'm sorry. You weren't exactly available for consultation."

Yont grew defensive. "He wasn't a yokel. He was really nice," her face grew beet red, "and now he's going to think I'm . . . I'm that way."

Weston watched her friend's face. There was so much going on—fury, sadness, anxiety flickered across it. Weston put out her hand to grasp Yont's. "No, he won't. Especially if you take the time to explain the situation to him. If he's as nice as you say, he'll understand."

Yont wrenched herself free of Weston's grasp. "No he won't, cause I'll never get to see him again." She turned and stormed out of the stairwell before Weston could reply. Weston watched the door close and thought, I can't go out there. There is a whole barracks full of women on the other side of that door, and they will all be looking for a fight. She lifted her shoulders toward her ears, trying to stretch the kink out of her neck. Shit, it hurt. She looked at her watch. Only three more hours till dinner. If she was extremely careful, she might survive till then.

Weston opened the door and walked through. She poked her head into the first cubicle she reached and said to none of the women in particular, "Inspection tomorrow. If you have any questions, ask me before chow tonight cause I'm hitting the sack right after. O.K.?" She didn't wait for their reply. Weston tromped along the corridor, making her little announcement and not bothering to wait for questions. It was her duty to remind them, so she was doing her duty. She had no great desire to do even that, but at least they couldn't say they hadn't been warned. At Bates' cube, she hadn't even finished blurting her reminder when Bates cut her off.

"Oh great, just who I want to see. Come here." Bates was standing in front of her locker fussing with the contents. Weston hesitated in the doorway and then grudgingly crossed the cube. "I bought a couple of things in Lancaster yesterday that aren't exactly regulation, but kind of are. Can you help me figure out how to stow them for inspection tomorrow?" Bates looked at Weston and smiled.

Weston looked from Bates to her locker shelf and back at Bates again. "You mean to tell me that you are spending the afternoon preparing for inspection? You haven't passed a single inspection since we've been here because you always just throw your stuff in."

"Wes," Bates pouted dramatically, "that's so unfair. You've been hounding me for weeks about the importance of each individual's effort at our weekly inspections, and now that I decide to turn over a new leaf, you're mean about it." She sniffed loudly for emphasis.

Weston was instantly contrite. "Oh, look, I'm sorry." She put her hand on Bates' shoulder. "I'm just a little grumpy today. You really have had a change of heart? What happened?"

Bates shrugged. "I don't know. There was something about yesterday in Lancaster. There I was in my new uniform, walking around, looking in shop windows, paying for everything with my own money, and getting a certain kind of . . . ," she paused a minute and looked at Weston carefully, "you're gonna think this is really dumb."

Weston frowned at her. "No, I won't. Go on."

Bates pursed her lips as if deciding if she could trust Weston. "Well, for the first time in my life I felt like I got a little respect. You know, from the shopkeepers and stuff." Bates took a deep breath. "For the first time in my life I felt like I was more than just a pair of big tits." She turned back to her locker. "So, help me find places to stash this stuff."

Weston continued to observe Bates for another long moment, and then smiled. "*Great*. So, what'd you buy that's off limits?"

Bates began pulling things from her locker. Weston named the items as Bates handed them to her. "Batteries, lipstick, cold cream . . . , um, nice undies." She held them up with one hand, her other full of Bates' belongings. "What's this?"

Bates retrieved the underwear. "Um, new toothbrush holder. I've stenciled the new undies. What about the other stuff?"

Weston dumped her armful of stuff on to Bates' bunk. "Well, scuttlebutt has it that they always ding you for something. But make sure it's all labeled clearly." She picked up the toothbrush holder again. "Weird shape, don't you think?"

Bates took it gently from her hand and put it back on the pile. "The guy I was with yesterday says it's kind of aerodynamic." She picked up the holder and a toothbrush and tiny tube of paste. "See, you can fit both in at once." She twisted the cap back on to the blunt end of the holder.

"Ugly color. Not really pink, but not really white either. Couldn't you find anything better?" Weston frowned.

"Not in this model, and this was the one I wanted," Bates stated matter-of-factly. "So, where should I stow it?"

"Just put it on the top shelf along with your other toiletries."

"Can't. Regs state *one* toothbrush and paste. I now have two of each."

Weston looked at her in surprise. "The regs state? Oh, never mind. Label it and stick it in your ditty bag. It's pretty safe."

Bates shook her head. "No. I don't want to. Don't want to risk a search." She paused, "You know how Kiel picks on me. I'd rather risk the barracks M.A.A."

"Well, fuck it. You seem to have all the answers," Weston was clearly exasperated. "You're going to a lot of effort for a goddamned toothbrush holder. You tell me where you're going to put it." She turned around to leave.

"Oh come on, Wes. I'll put it in the bottom of my laundry bag, O.K.?"

Weston nodded in agreement. "O.K. But leave the M.A.A. something in your locker she can pick up on first." Weston thought a moment. "Maybe the spare batteries in your dress shoes. Only partially hidden. That way she'll think she's got you and probably not even check the laundry bag."

Weston strolled out of the cube, then turned at the doorway. "Hey, Bates?"

"Yeah?"

"Welcome aboard, and don't worry too much about tomorrow. I hear they're usually pretty easy the first inspection after liberty." She turned and finished her tour through the barracks.

23

Another pissy, cold, rainy day. The company entered the barracks after classes and began removing galoshes and raincoats. Some hung about the lounge pulling cigarettes from their ditty bags and collapsing on the worn sofas. It almost felt good to be back in the routine that they knew and loathed. Almost. Weston and Taylor were just passing the watch station when one of the women on duty called to them.

"Weston? Taylor?"

"Yeah," they both replied in unison, suspicion weighting their voices.

"Don't get comfortable. The C.C. wants to see both of you over at the drillhall." She added as an afterthought, "Before evening mess."

The three women exchanged glances, and then Weston and Taylor struggled back into their raincoats. "Shit," Weston groaned. "I can think of about six thousand things she'll want to yell at us for."

Taylor smiled ruefully. "Attitude problem, Weston. What makes you think we're not being called before our dutiful C.C. for a commendation of merit?" Taylor buttoned her coat. "Shall we have a quick smoke now, or get this over with and then dope up before dinner?"

"Oh, ugh," Weston made strangling motions with her hands around her own throat, "let's go get it over with. O.K.?"

The two women tromped back through the rain, across the grinder, and into the drillhall. A fissure of light splayed along the horizon, but overhead, underfoot, and all around it was the gray, soggy twilight of a raw spring day. They stepped into the drillhall and were enveloped in dusk. They stamped their feet and removed their overcoats and hung them on pegs. They marched down the broad side of the building, the echo of their steps sounding before and behind them. At the C.C.'s office they stopped, looked briefly at each other, and then took a deep breath.

"Recruits Weston and Taylor reporting as ordered," Weston said loudly, clearly, standing just outside the C.C.'s doorway.

For a moment, all that could be heard was the rustling of papers. Then the scraping of a chair as it was moved across the floorboards. "Enter."

The two women entered the office and stood at attention in front of P.O. Langhard's desk, and waited. She shuffled papers and tidied her desk.

"This will only take a moment, ladies. But I warn you not to let the brevity of our visit leave you with the impression that the issues we will discuss today are not important. It is the small details of discipline on which one builds one's commands."

"Seaman recruit Taylor." Weston saw the woman next to her visibly stiffen. "As company cadence caller you have been entrusted with a certain degree of authority. The first duty of any officer is to always ensure that the implementation of that authority reflects in a positive manner on themselves, on their command, and on the military." Langhard paused to let her words sink in on the two recruits before her. The two young women waited anxiously, their breathing gone short and shallow.

164

Langhard folded her hands on the desk top and continued. "It has been brought to my attention that on Saturday, March 3, you did willfully use a call for company cadence that had been declared off limits. This unfortunate error on your part was compounded by the fact that it happened in the presence of the most junior company in this command." Langhard sighed heavily. "Seaman recruit Taylor, let me take this opportunity to remind you that as cadence caller it is your duty to inspire your company to do its best." She pointed her index finger at Taylor. "At the same time, senior companies must always set an example to the new recruits on board." She pushed her chair away and stood behind the desk. "Enough said. This won't happen again, will it Taylor?

Taylor swallowed before replying a firm, "No, ma'am."

Langhard walked around the desk and closed a second door to her office that led into a warren of offices and work spaces. She brushed by Weston and returned to her chair behind the desk.

"Seaman recruit Weston." The recruit could feel her heartbeat skip-jump in tempo, a flush creep over her face. "The master M.A.A. of the recruit barracks has seen fit to bring to my attention a number of irregularities she discovered in the course of your routine barracks inspection this morning." The C.C. bent down and began removing items from her desk drawer while she continued speaking. "And while as company M.A.A. you cannot be aware of all the contraband other recruits may bring into the barracks, especially after their first shore leave...."

Weston watched as Langhard dropped a half-pound box of chocolates onto her desk. It was followed by a sheaf of movie star magazines, a couple of paperback novels, a yo-yo, a harmonica, a small teddy bear, a box of Ritz dye for clothing, and a six-pack of beer. "But the sheer number of items confiscated from your company quarters this morning," Weston could now hear a distinct but muted hum emanating from Langhard's desk, "leads me to believe that perhaps you have failed to stress to your recruits the seriousness of being caught with contraband in their belongings." At this point the C.C. produced what looked to Weston like Bates' toothbrush holder. Langhard slammed it onto the desk top to emphasize her final statement and, as if by magic, it began to rotate of its own accord in a small circle amongst the array of items. Like a totem, it rose amidst the debris and hummed.

Weston's eyes widened in surprise and disbelief. Next to her, Taylor was making choking noises in her throat. The small woman's whole body shook perceptibly. Weston returned her attention to the company commander.

"Seaman recruit Weston," Langhard bellowed, "do you know what this IS?" *This* could only be reference to the shimmying cylinder in the middle of the CC's desk.

Weston held her breath and replied, "I believe it's Bates' new toothbrush holder, ma'am." She looked her commander directly in the eye. Taylor's breathing had gone ragged and raspy. She was beginning to snort.

Langhard held Weston's gaze for what felt like an eternity. Finally, she leaned over and cleared the top of her desk with one sweeping motion of her chunky forearm. "I think, recruit Weston, that for future inspections—" There was a short knock on the door of Langhard's office.

"Recruit petty officer Kiel, reporting as ordered, ma'am."

"Stand aside, Kiel," Langhard called back. "I'm just finishing up here."

"Aye, aye."

Langhard returned her attention to Weston. "As I was saying, impress on your recruits the seriousness of both the company barracks inspections *and* the whole issue of contraband." She raised her hand and pointed to the drillhall beyond her office door. "Parade rest outside my office. Both of you, now." She sat back in her chair, effectively dismissing them.

The two women did an impeccable about-face and marched out of the office. They lined up against the wall at attention, widened their stances, and clasped their hands behind their backs. Each stared straight ahead. Kiel passed them as she, in turn, entered the C.C.'s office. The door closed behind her. Out of the corner of her eye Weston could see Taylor's face, a grin creased it from ear to ear, and every few seconds she snuffed and huffed with suppressed laughter. The sounds of muted conversation flowed from beneath the door and through the transom.

Quite suddenly the door opened, and Langhard and Kiel emerged together. They passed the two women without a word to either of them and turned and strolled down the drillhall. Weston followed their progress for as long as she could out of the corner of her eye. Langhard was lecturing Kiel, marking some important point she was expressing by karate chopping the air with the edge of her hand. And then they disappeared.

Silence reigned, except for the sporadic chuffing from the woman next to her. Weston could hear doors closing somewhere distant in the drillhall. The crunch of automobile tires on gravel sounded from outside. R.T.C.W. staff must have cars, drive to work, lead other lives than those she saw here. The thought startled Weston with its obviousness. She had honestly never thought of them as human beings interacting as human beings somewhere beyond this realm. She shoved that thought aside, promising herself she would come back to it. But there was always so much to think about in the few moments of quiet she was handed each day that she hated to squander it all on only one topic. There were so many things that needed examining, questioning, assimilating. Weston never felt like she quite managed it all.

"Tell me the truth, Weston. Did you really think that the contraption Bates showed you was a toothbrush holder?" Taylor's husky voice seeped into Weston's reverie.

There was a long moment of silence before Weston replied, "That's what she said it was."

"But what did *your* gut tell you, girl?" Taylor sounded exasperated.

Another long silence ensued. Weston could hear the both of them breathing. The furnace, somewhere, clicked on filling the vast reaches of the arena around her with a low pulsing noise. It was perfect accompaniment to the dusk that blanketed the windows.

"That she was lying," Weston paused. "Maybe because I grew up in a family that spent a lot of energy pretending my dad wasn't a drunk, and lying about when he was. I have developed this radar, an ultrasensitivity to lying."

Taylor snorted, "I'd say it's a good thing, too." She paused and then added. "So you knew Bates was lying, trying to pawn a dildo off on you as a toothbrush holder. Why didn't you call her on it?"

Weston ducked her head and examined her shoes. She sighed. "Habit, partially. At home, whenever anyone—Mom, Dad, or even one of my sisters—was lying to save Dad's ass, no one ever blew the whistle." She looked up at Taylor quickly and then continued, "You just stood tough and hung together."

Weston cleared her throat. "Denying I know anything about sex is a habit, too." She laughed. "I mean, I grew up in a family of five girls. I'm sure my mom figured, as we all neared adolescence, that she was better off telling us nothing about sex. Just to mention the word was enough to give her nightmares about a house full of unwed mothers."

Taylor's eyes brightened, and she laughed too. "So, how did you find out the essentials?" She paused for emphasis. "I mean, you do know the essentials? Don't you?

"Taylor," Weston's voice was scornful, "sure, I know." A smile lit up her face. "I went to the public library." Laughingly, "I've always said anything you wanted to know is in the public library."

"You read about dildos in the library?" Taylor's voice was incredulous.

Weston's face colored. "Well, no. I started reading men's magazines in college, you know. All the girls who were liberated did. Anyway, I read about them in Xaveria Hollander's sex advice column." A grin spread across her face. "I mean, look at it this way. I'd never actually seen one before. So I wasn't about to stand there and accuse Bates of lying *and* trying to hide a dildo in the barracks." She shrugged. "I figured if I kept my mouth shut, the barracks M.A.A. would take care of it." Weston winked at Taylor. "I would've loved to have seen her face when she pulled that out of the duffel bag." Both women broke up at the thought.

Once they had sobered, Taylor whispered, "Don't be too

hard on Bates." She stared straight ahead, once again at parade rest. "Trusting people comes in steps."

Weston punched Taylor lightly in the arm. "O.K., mom. Whatever you say."

Taylor's voice grew rough and clipped. "Yeah, well I don't know why its always *me* that winds up telling you this shit. And don't forget, you're supposed to be at parade rest."

Silence for a moment. "You know she's gone off and left us. She's forgotten we're here." The *she* Taylor was referring to was their C.C. The absolute quiet in the drillhall underscored her comment.

"I don't much care, except that I don't want to miss chow." Weston's stomach grumbled along with her.

"Let's give her five more minutes," Taylor continued, "and if she doesn't show, we'll boogey."

Weston peeked at her watch. "I don't know. We're in trouble now."

"You gonna stand here all night just because that cow went off and left us?" Taylor's temper was instantaneous. "It was probably on purpose, Wes. Her idea of punishment." Taylor's toe started to tap in irritation.

Weston sighed, "O.K. Five minutes." They waited, Taylor's foot tapping, the distant furnace humming. But it was no longer pleasant. They both felt abandoned.

"God, it's quiet. I'll bet there ain't a soul left in here but us." Taylor's harsh whisper startled Weston. "I'm thinking that this might be the perfect opportunity to do a little detective work." Taylor rubbed her hands together and fell out of line.

"Where are you going?" Weston's voice was laden with suspicion as she watched Taylor cross in front of her and enter the C.C.'s office.

"Never you mind. Just keep your eyes and ears wide open and if you see or hear anything, I want you to cough real loud and I'll beetle on out of here." Taylor closed the office door, leaving a crack open to make sure she would hear Weston's signal. "If it's an emergency, you just say nice and loud, 'Good evening, ma'am.' I'll take off through the other door and circle back around." Taylor looked Weston directly in the eyes. "I'm in here looking for a bathroom, Weston. Do try to believe that, O.K.?" She disappeared completely.

Weston shook her head, "You little creep. That's the last time I pour my heart out to you."

Taylor's response was unintelligible from inside Langhard's office. Weston tried to follow her progress through the small sounds she heard coming from the room. There was the ponderous roll of a file cabinet drawer being opened, then the heavy clunk of it being shut. Another one rolled open. At the same time her mind went into overdrive trying to process all the myriad noises that suddenly seemed to fill the empty drillhall. Because it was empty she told herself. Empty. Weston closed her eyes to concentrate. Shit. Don't close your eyes, you fool, she screamed at herself.

"Well, do tell. The navy keeps some interesting stuff on file." Another protracted silence, then Taylor spoke again. "Your file was easy to find. Hoo-ee, looks like you better be buying some suntan lotion, kid. You're going to photo school." The joy in Taylor's voice was genuine. "Guess it pays to tweak them dagger's tits," her voice boomed from the office.

"Would you hurry up? Don't you think you're pushing your luck in there?" All of Weston's anxiety had suddenly returned. Weston forced her eyes to scan the four corners of the drillhall. No one. Yet.

"Just a minute more. I'm not in the drawer." Weston could hear another file drawer being shut. "I'm just gonna check the desk top." Silence. "See, I told you. Langhard's got a list of academic standings for every week at bootcamp. Who do you think was top of the list every damned week?" Taylor laughed to herself in triumph. "Won't that get Kiel's neat little butt to find out she got aced by a colored girl?" Taylor peeked through the doorway at Weston. "That's not all."

"Jesus, Taylor. Come on." There was definite panic in Weston's voice.

"Just one second more. I want to find the personnel report." Taylor disappeared. Weston breathed a momentary sigh

of relief. "They said they recommend me highly for ATC school."
A raucous laugh filtered through the crack in the doorway. Then,
more silence, protracted silence, interminable silence. Weston
waited. She heard the slap of the file folder hitting. . .what? The
desk top. The office door swung open and a grim-faced Taylor
pushed her way past Weston and kept walking.

"Taylor wait. What is it?" Weston immediately started after
her. She ran and caught the small woman just before she exited the drillhall. Weston grabbed her arm. "Taylor, what's wrong?
Taylor." Weston forced herself between the recruit and the doorway. "You're not getting out of here until you tell me what
happened."

"Langhard's dismissed the personnel report." Taylor's voice
was a monotone. "She cited today's reprimand as an example.
Fuck, I should have known she would just be waiting for something she could document." Taylor pushed Weston aside roughly.
"I'm not going to school after bootcamp because of that fucking incident on the grinder with Hernandez." The anguish in her
voice hung in the air long after she had disappeared through
the doorway.

Weston caught a movement out of the corner of her eye
and turned to the nearest window. In that second, Taylor's head
and shoulders were framed by the white window frame and sash.
Cold evening drizzle beaded on her hat brim and glittered on
the shoulders of her coat. From the set of her shoulders Weston
could tell her hands would be clenched into fists. Tight black
fists that matched Taylor's jawline. Weston closed her eyes against
the picture. Even a millisecond was too much.

24

Weston hadn't talked to Taylor in days. They seemed to be taking turns avoiding each other. It wasn't hard if neither of them worked to circumvent navy rules and regulations. They could easily finish out bootcamp without talking again. For the first time, Weston became aware of just how much effort it took from both of them to make their friendship work.

After spending several days uncertain how to approach Taylor, or even what to say, Weston was growing more and more desperate to talk. She expended an inordinate amount of energy trying to decipher Taylor's mood from the cadences she called. Was now a good time to broach the subject? Would Taylor ever be willing to discuss her feelings with Weston? It seemed that just when Weston was most inclined to throw caution to the wind and confront Taylor, she invariably got signals that to do so would be disastrous.

After the first week of exile, Weston had decided to do her late-night thinking in bed. They had begun standing watches in four-hour shifts during the night, and it was getting more difficult dragging herself to the washroom to keep her increasingly lonely vigil. It seemed as if no one had anything to say anymore. She knew she had been too abrupt with Bates lately and was making her feel unwelcome. Yont had quit coming to the washroom at night entirely. Weston realized with a shock one night that after all her complaining to Taylor about needing time to herself, she now had too much. She felt completely isolated, and, ironically, the rigid military structure she hated had become a comfort.

During the day, Taylor spent what free time she had with Jones. While they had seemed to have such a hard time relating in the past, now, if she wasn't careful, Weston was sure to run into them in the lounge. They'd be deep in conversation, or sitting and smoking and laughing with Harper as the silent observer. At least it made it simple: she could easily avoid all three.

Sometimes Weston had intense conversations with herself, playing both Taylor and herself. They would accidentally bump into each other in the washroom late one night. Taylor would be smoking, and Weston would take a cigarette nonchalantly and join her. There would be a kind of long uncomfortable silence, but finally Taylor would say something bitchy. Well, not bitchy exactly, but she wouldn't make it easy.

At this point, Weston's make-believe always faltered. What she realized is that she didn't know how to act or what to say in this situation. How could she tell Taylor she was sorry the world's a racist place? Should she apologize for getting what she wanted when Taylor didn't? It was such a dirty little lie that they had uncovered, and neither one of them wanted to be the first to bring it up for discussion. There were times when she was tempted to follow Taylor till she caught her alone and then harass her, make her talk. She wanted to shake her and demand to know how she could let this stand between them being friends. Weston wanted to shout at her, *Just because the navy is stupid, just because you're angry, doesn't mean we can't be friends.* The reason Weston never acted on these impulses was because in her heart-of-hearts she was secretly afraid it really did mean they couldn't be friends. Rather than know that for certain, she chose not to act at all.

Days had gone by and then a week. Weston dressed quickly, quietly, in the soft glow of the exit sign. She had ten minutes to finish dressing, rush to the washroom, and race upstairs to her duty station. Standing watch from midnight to 0400 hours was not her idea of a good time. It seemed like she spent the whole four hours watching the clock, willing the minute hand to shrug its way around the perimeter. She pulled her sweater from the top shelf and heard a soft *thunk* as something hit the floor. Weston bent down and ran her hands along the foot of the locker. There. She grasped the object and held it up to the dim light. A spool of navy-blue thread. She turned as she pulled on her sweater, and her eyes flickered to Yont's bunk. She hadn't come back from watch yet. Weston sighed. Eight p.m.-to-midnight didn't seem to be nearly as bad a shift. She hoped Yont was managing to stay awake. She plunked the thread back on the shelf and quietly closed the locker door.

Weston hurried to the watch station on her floor and checked herself out of her company's quarters. She stated her destination and then bolted for the washroom. Quick to the latrine. Splash water on your face. Replace your glasses and race for the stairs. Up two flights and report to the other watch station to begin her duty. At least with all the running around before her watch began, she started out wide awake.

"Weston, R. D. reporting for duty." She whispered to the woman behind the station bulkhead. The recruit dutifully opened the station log book and signed Weston's name and time of arrival.

"You've got a minute before your duty actually commences. Do you want me to wait?" The woman's sleepy voice was laced with hope. A minute was forever.

Weston shook her head. "Don't be silly. Go to bed. Who's on with me tonight?"

The other recruit smiled her thanks. "Someone from the first floor, named Franklin. Hasn't shown yet." The recruit gathered her ditty bag and cap. "My watch partner said she'd hang around for another ten minutes till she shows. She's off on rounds and will be back in a minute." Weston moved behind the desk in the station. "Night," the other recruit called softly as she left.

Weston sighed and seated herself in the swivel chair. Two hundred and thirty-nine minutes to go. Her partner's ditty bag peered out at her from the shadows beyond the corner of the desk. God, who would voluntarily stay an extra ten minutes of any watch, anywhere in the whole U.S. Navy? She reached for the ditty bag and pulled it toward her, into the light.

"Now you know everything in that bag is stenciled, per regulations. There's no need to be checking up on me." The voice with its sweet southern drawl was unmistakable.

Weston couldn't help herself, her grin was broad, welcoming, as the other woman edged into the watch station and leaned against the wall near her chair. "I suppose you expect that I'll just take your word for that." Weston tapped the ditty bag. "It seems to me you're one of the blessed few who has totally escaped a snap inspection, so far." She cocked her head toward the recruit. "Correct me if I'm wrong."

Harper chuckled as she propped a foot against the desk edge. "Well, if you're going to be rooting around in there, dig out my cigarettes and lighter while you're at it." She took them carefully from Weston's outstretched hand. "Join me."

"Thanks." Weston lit her cigarette and inhaled. "You want to pull up the other chair?" she whispered to Harper.

"Yeah. Don't forget to enter in the log that I did my rounds." She gently pushed another chair next to Weston's.

Weston made a notation that Harper had checked all the cubicles and exits. She neatly printed the time and the standard phrase, *All is well.* Damn, how could five minutes have passed so easily? She quickly looked at her wristwatch to double-check the time. "Should I make a notation about Franklin being late for her duty?"

"Maybe. Not yet. Let's wait and see what happens." Harper sat down.

Weston was afraid to look up from the log book to meet

Harper's eyes. She felt the hair along the back of her neck prickle. What did Harper mean? They were sitting awfully close— wouldn't someone notice? Suddenly she felt sick and excited the way she used to feel standing in line for the ferris wheel at the state fair. She had always known then that nothing could really happen to her, the rides were perfectly safe, but she could make herself giddy with anticipation that was almost better than the ride. Weston felt a hot flush color her cheeks.

"You're awfully quiet. Maybe I should just go." Harper made no move to leave her chair.

"No." The word was out before Weston could rephrase it. "I mean, you don't have to. It'd be nice to just sit," Weston's eyes met Harper's, "and talk."

Harper smiled a slow, easy-going grin. "Yeah, I thought so too." She flicked a bit of ash off the tip of her cigarette. And waited.

Weston ran the tip of the pen up and down the zipper on her ditty bag. She should say something but she didn't know what. She hardly knew anything at all about Harper. Now would be the perfect time to ask. Somehow all the questions that popped into her mind seemed so banal. The things she really wanted to know were unsayable. She couldn't compose them as explicit questions, even in her mind. She sat fiddling with her ink pen, wanting to know everything, yet lacking the words to begin. So she picked a different topic.

"How much do you know about why Taylor isn't talking to me?"

Harper smiled slightly and exhaled a puff of smoke. They sat shoulder to shoulder behind the watch station desk, their voices mere rustlings on the wind to the sleeping women sur-rounding them. She leaned across Weston and tapped her cig-arette into the ashtray on the desk. "I know it's hard not to per-sonalize it. But if you think back on the week, you'll see that Taylor hasn't been talking to anyone. Except Amanda. Certainly not to me."

Harper leaned back against the chair. "I've overheard enough to know that she managed to do some snooping around and has somehow found out she won't be going to air traffic control school. Unless we witness an act of God." She put a hand on Weston's shoulder. "It's been hard, huh?"

Weston nodded. "For different reasons. I hadn't realized how much I depended on her to make this place bearable. In her own way she's been really nice to me, and now this happens. Even if I knew what to say, she won't let me near her. I want to help somehow, and she's just turned right off me."

Harper nodded in turn. "Yeah, sometimes the hardest thing in the world to give someone you care for is the space to come around and let you care. It's hard to wait them out."

"Maybe she won't come around."

"Maybe she won't." Harper took a drag on her cigarette. "The second hardest thing in the world to do is accept that everything in this life is a time-limited offer." She exhaled slowly. "This is pure speculation, Weston, but maybe this is as far as Taylor can go. Maybe she's not ready to trust anyone white, Black, or otherwise any further than she's trusted you. And this is her way out."

Weston sat bolt upright. "What—"

"Ssh, not so loud." Harper's hand smothered the rest of Weston's sentence. "I said it was just guessing on my part." Harper began her defense. "I'm just saying, maybe. But you two were pretty intense. Hell, the whole first five weeks of bootcamp has been pretty intense. Maybe Taylor just needed a breather from it all." She pushed Weston back in her chair. "Remember what it was like when you were ten? And you found a new friend at school. I'll bet you spent every free second with them. Didn't you?"

Weston's eyes widened. "Yeah. My mom was always telling me to slow down, ease up. I didn't have to do it all in one day. How'd you know?"

Harper chuckled, "That's what you two have been like. Taylor's tough-guy act was so transparent. She needed you as much as you needed her, but in different ways. Maybe she just needs some time to see that."

Weston sat up again and searched Harper's face with her

eyes. "Yeah? You really think so?"

Harper leaned forward and stubbed out her cigarette. "Maybe. Maybe so." She turned and caught Weston's eyes with her own. Their faces were so close in the dark that Weston could taste the cigarette on Harper's breath. There was a smile harbored deep in the green eyes. Without explanation, Weston moved as naturally as if she kissed women every day of the week and closed the gap between their mouths. She watched Harper's eyes close as she placed her hand behind her head and pulled her mouth even closer. There was a moment's hesitation, and then Harper's tongue reached for hers. Weston refused to close her eyes, needing to commit to memory the beauty of Harper's brows and cheeks and eyes. For the first time in her life she had a feeling that anticipation would pale compared to the ride.

Harper gently pulled away. She sat and looked at Weston silently, a smile touching the corners of her mouth. "I guess it's time I went and found the other watch." She rose slowly from her chair. "There's sure to be hell to pay if I don't." She tucked her ditty bag under one arm and jammed her cap on her head. "Don't forget to log me out." Harper leaned over and swiftly placed a kiss on Weston's mouth before she breezed from the watch station.

25

Like the security camera suspended from the ceiling in the bank, Weston replayed the scene with Harper over and over again. In her mind's eye it had been filmed from over her left shoulder in grainy black and white. She watched as it unreeled in her sleep. There. There was the exact moment. Stop. Stop the film. In her sleep she zeroed in on the frame where she had leaned forward and kissed Harper. She turned to the women assembled behind her as if to say, *See.*

They nodded their heads collectively. Indeed, they did see. She was the one who had kissed Harper, not the other way around. They nodded their heads again knowingly. Not a single face expressed shock. Weston's eyes searched every face in turn. Her grandmother's was as usual, a soft smile and eyes that registered love, concern. Mrs. Norcross, her first-grade teacher, looked harried but not surprised. And so it went down the line, every woman that she had ever loved and trusted. No one seemed surprised but Weston.

After the initial euphoria wore off, Weston's normally active mind clicked into overdrive. During the day she was determined to concentrate only on her duties and her studies. Nothing else. But at night, the moment she was asleep, her mind brought out the film clips of all the times she had ever been close to other women.

What about the time in seventh grade? She was standing outside the gym with her best friend waiting for the class bell to ring, signaling them to proceed to the next class. She had her books tucked under one arm and was holding hands with her friend with her free hand. As the bell rang and the other students began to straggle off to the next class, the gym teacher called to them. She haltingly informed them that they were, perhaps, too old to be still holding hands. That was something first graders did. It didn't look right. Weston and her friend were suitably embarrassed and never did it again. But Weston missed that feeling of closeness nonetheless.

Or the time Janice Turner's mom caught them "practice kissing" in the backyard one summer night they decided to have a sleepout. Even then, Weston knew on some level that that was the reason she and Janice stopped being friends. Not because Janice didn't like the kissing. But because her mom disapproved.

She always thought she had bypassed the stage of high school crushes all her friends went through. She could even admit to feeling a little self-righteous as she counseled them through their crises. Life with an alcoholic might be hell, but it had given her a maturity her peers lacked. While they were still learning their emotional ABCs, she had gotten to skip a grade, so to speak. But in the end she succumbed to loneliness. There was only so much gratification to be gained from being above it all, and she had come to feel a little cheated by her inability to fall in love. What she wanted, after all, was to just be normal. To feel the thrill of meeting someone, to fall in love, and even to experience the agony when it didn't work out. In her sleep, Weston came to realize that she had been doing this all along. The list of her loves was as lengthy and varied as the dreams that troubled her. By night she visited them again and again, and by day she was bothered by their emotional residue.

Once again she was restless. A dream had awakened her, left her with its aftermath, but given her no explanations. She tried lying on her side, first one then the other. She turned on her back, then flipped over to her stomach. She dangled her foot off the edge of the bunk and twiddled it until her ankle hurt and the woman below her complained that she was shaking the bunk. Weston rolled over, pounded her pillow, and stuffed it under her head. Pretend you're asleep. Breathe deep and slow the way you do when you first start falling. Let your jaw go slack. Don't keep it tight like that. Close your eyes and really feel your heart rate drop. Finally, everyone else in her cube was asleep but her. Weston climbed from the bunk and padded on bare feet to the washroom.

She pushed open the washroom door, and the light hit her full out, like the beam from a freight train that freezes creatures in its path.

"Didn't think you'd ever show up. Get in here and shut the damn door."

With eyes still clamped shut, Weston felt her way toward the counter top where she knew Taylor would be sitting. With one hand on the wall and the other on the formica, she heaved herself up and then slid along till her back was solidly against the mirror. She drew her knees up to her chest and pulled her nightgown down over them for warmth. Balancing her elbows on her knees, Weston used her hand to shield her eyes so that she could see Taylor's face. They studied each other a long time.

"Well, don't think I'm gonna do all the talking," Taylor said accusingly. "Cause I ain't."

"Don't know what to say," Weston started, doubtful. "You mad at me?"

Taylor took a deep drag on her cigarette and then slid the package across the counter to Weston. "You tell me."

Weston took a long time selecting her cigarette, lighting it, and then took some more time just looking at the package. "Um, I think that maybe you're not really mad at me, in particular.

But that it's hard to separate a system that isn't fair from the ones who seem to benefit from it." Weston had been staring at her cigarette but looked over at Taylor for some signal.

"You figure that, do you?" Taylor's tone was noncommittal.

Weston began again, her tone earnest. "I know it doesn't do any good, but I'm sorry. You're ten times smarter than me in a lot of ways, and you deserve a chance." Weston set her jaw and waited for Taylor to get mad at her for expressing pity, when it wasn't that at all. She was just sorry.

"Sorry ain't worth a heap of shit, honey." Taylor said it softly, with a certain resignation. "What are we gonna do about it?" she demanded. "You're so sorry. Would you give me your school if you could?" Taylor's voice was harsh, unreadable.

Weston took a long drag on her cigarette. "No, Taylor, I wouldn't. I'll make a good photographer." Weston watched the other woman's eyes closely and then added, "But if I knew anything else that would help, I'd do it." Each held the other's gaze for a long time.

Taylor coughed and then spoke. "Well, I never had much use for doormats. Just clutter up the floor." She stubbed out her cigarette and pulled a wrinkled envelope from the pocket of her robe. "My Uncle Roy wrote. He said there's more than one way to skin a cat. As long as I get myself assigned to an airbase with a control tower, I can work my way into their school." She smiled and sighed. "A bunch of them are coming down from the City for graduation."

Very carefully, Weston measured out the silence between them. "Can I meet them?"

Taylor's face grew fierce. Just as quickly the anger passed. "That's why I wanted to tell you now. I need them to myself." She paused, "There'd be so much explaining to do. You to them. Them to you. I don't want to be no one's interpreter." Taylor's eyes dropped to the package of cigarettes on the counter. "It's energy I don't have any more."

Harper's voice played at the back of Weston's mind, "The second hardest thing in the world to accept is that everything in this life is a time-limited offer." Weston nodded in silent agreement and reached out and grasped Taylor's hand, held it as they both sat in silence for the moment. "That's O.K., Taylor. You know, we got each other this far."

Taylor squeezed Weston's hand in reply. They sat a moment longer and then Weston slowly pushed herself off the counter. She started for the washroom door.

"You coming?"

"Not just yet," Taylor yawned. "I'm gonna have one more smoke." She waved her hand at Weston, "Go on, get going." Weston turned to leave.

"Roberta." Weston had nearly walked through the doorway before she recognized that Taylor was talking to her.

She turned and smiled broadly, "Yeah, Cecelia."

"I don't ever want to see you smoke another cigarette, you hear?" Taylor's voice was laden with sarcasm. "It ain't good for you. Besides, you do it so badly, it's painful to watch." She matched Weston's smile. "Now, get on to bed."

Weston laughed and pushed her way out of the washroom. "O.K., I promise."

26

Suddenly, the days had no meaning. They all knew that they were only marking time while final grades were compiled, orders were cut, and the grand finale on graduation day was enacted. They were the senior company and the thought made Weston laugh. She vividly remembered her first view of the senior company that first day in camp. They had seemed so grand, so in charge, so together as they marched through that cold January morning. Weston's company was anything but together. Like a poor marriage, they presented a solid enough front to the world, but bickered continually behind closed doors.

It had seemed as if at precisely the same moment, every woman in the company realized the navy would never flunk them now. On the morning of their final barracks inspection, Weston was so exasperated all she could do was laugh. While every other company in the history of the Recruit Training Center for Women had killed themselves to make sure that every cube passed, had goaded themselves into proving that their quarters were the ultimate, had bought the ticket that as the senior company every bunk and passageway must be perfect, every locker immaculate, Weston's company did only what it had to and no more. They got their pennant anyway. This was what nearly did Weston in. As the barracks M.A.A. handed her the pennant after the inspection, Weston almost strangled trying not to laugh. She immediately handed it over to Yont, who held it reverently.

"Quit looking at that rag like it was the academy award, will you?" Weston sounded sharper than she meant to be with Yont.

"Look, just because you think it's corny, don't try to take away my pride in being able to carry this our last week at camp." Yont was defensive.

"But it's such a joke. You know as well as I do that we didn't earn that thing." Weston was becoming far too emotional, considering the subject matter, but she couldn't seem to rein herself in now that she had started. "This company never had a single inspection where we all passed." She wiped her brow with the back of her hand. "You know that better than anybody."

Yont turned and faced Weston squarely. "I don't know about you, but I earned this sucker. I earned it with every single day I spent here, with every time I had to listen to women bickering all around me. Arguments that no one would ever win because neither side would ever listen to the other." Her eyes flashed as she talked, her face grown fierce and hawklike. "You go ahead and stand on principle, Weston. But I'm gonna go ahead and take every little doodad they want to give me—and still it won't be enough. Nothing will ever make up for the time I spent here." She turned away and stomped back to their quarters with the flag fluttering gently over her shoulder.

Weston suspected that Yont was as near tears as she was at this moment. What had they all expected that they now felt so disappointed? She had begun to ask herself this question late at night when she lay in her bunk thinking. Initially she believed it might be like her relationships with her sisters at home, only more so. Easier in a lot of ways, because new people are often nicer to friends than they are to family.

But in bootcamp it seemed you got the worst of the familiarity that family brings without the benefit of any of the good stuff thrown in to lighten the going. Weston mentally ran through a checklist of all the women she knew in her company and then tried to pair them up with a best friend. When it came right down to it, the only two she could think of were Jones and Harper, and they didn't count. After ten weeks she could not identify a single friendship that had blossomed at bootcamp.

That's not to say that Weston totally discounted her bootcamp relationships, especially with Taylor. If nothing else, the last two weeks had made it abundantly clear just how important they had been to each other. They had helped each other survive, although she still did not know exactly how or why. But surviving was not friendship, and the subtle difference haunted Weston and made her sad. Maybe, in fact, that was the answer, that they had all been different, too different. In the end, perhaps they all got as much as anyone could have gotten out of it. And they would just have to be satisfied with that.

Their final class in military protocol and procedures was preempted. They had all filed into the classroom as usual, sitting alphabetically as usual. The petty officer who generally conducted the class was a nervous, jumpy woman who Weston tried not to watch. It made her twitch in some kind of subconscious response. This afternoon she was more jittery than usual. Once they had taken their seats she began a brief introduction to the subject matter for the day.

"For the last nine weeks we have completed a rapid overview of some of the more important military customs such as saluting officers, asking permission to come aboard, and finer points of military etiquette. Many of the procedures we have discussed are courtesies, military manners, so to speak. Just as our society has differing levels of accepted behavior, so does the navy. Just as society has one set of rules that are left to the individual's discretion, like saying please and thank you, so does the navy. While saluting a superior officer is a custom, and every well-mannered sailor would oblige, the penalty for disobedience is not that severe.

"But there are some rules in the navy that sailors must obey or they will be imprisoned. Today an officer from the Judge Advocate General Corps is here to more thoroughly acquaint you with these rules." The petty officer finished her twittery speech just as the door opened and a woman lieutenant strode into the room.

All heads turned to follow her progress to the front of the room. The recruits didn't get to see officers much, and the ones they did see scared them to death. Unless they kept their caps on, Weston still had a hard time differentiating between real officers and the senior petty officers. It hadn't been two hours after their first lecture on how to distinguish the two and the proper way to salute that Weston had been in the drillhall. She was leading a small squad somewhere, and they had all seen the woman approaching, certain to pass them. As squad leader it was Weston's duty to extend the proper courtesy for them all.

There had ensued an energetic dialogue with all the squad members as to whether it was, indeed, an officer approaching. No one knew for sure. No one could remember whether it was customary to salute inside the drillhall or not. They discussed the worst thing that could happen if it was an officer and Weston didn't salute. Or, if it wasn't and she did. In the end they decided it was Weston's problem, and she could sort it out. All the while they had been marching. A split second before they drew abreast of each other, Weston made her decision. Up came her arm in a perfectly rendered military salute. Three steps later the whole squad breathed a huge sigh of relief. Four, five, six steps.

"Young lady," the woman's voice filled the drillhall to overflowing. The squad lurched to an immediate halt.

Weston had gambled that if the woman was not an officer, she would be flattered that Weston had assumed she was one, and let them pass. The gamble failed to pay off, but Weston never again had trouble spotting an officer on the loose.

This officer was young and very good-looking, or so Weston thought. She draped her tall, slim frame on the edge of the desk in a most unofficerly fashion. She started off her talk with things like the history of mutiny and the fate of mutineers. Then she proceeded to traitors, Benedict Arnold and the like. The kind of things that everyone knew no one in the room would really ever do. She went on to discuss the finer distinctions between absent without leave, or A.W.O.L., and desertion. Still stuff no one ever dreamed of doing.

The officer continued at some length describing the fairness of the navy's extensive judicial system, if a recruit ever had occasion to find herself in the midst of it. The navy would even provide her with a lawyer to defend herself, one of their own, if it ever came to that. It didn't occur to Weston at the time to question how committed a lawyer might be to her case if the same lawyer was being paid by the navy. Or whether the navy would be willing to pay a civilian lawyer that Weston liked better, if that were the case. No, for Weston good questions like these only arrived in her head once the opportunity had passed to express them.

The officer droned on and on. Weston had lost all interest in what she was saying, good-looking or not. She had launched her talk into a whole new area, but it was only the same old stuff they had heard before they had started standing watches at night. Don't sit on a bunk with another recruit. Don't ever be alone in a room with the door closed with only one other woman present. Don't touch. Don't kiss. Wait a minute—Weston sat upright. She didn't remember any petty officer ever saying don't kiss.

"Any of these acts, in varying circumstances, can or might be labeled unnatural—"

Near the middle of the room, seaman recruit Jones shot to her feet and stood at attention. It was the correct procedure for asking permission to speak.

"Seaman recruit Jones asking permission to speak, ma'am." Jones stared straight ahead.

The officer was obviously a little surprised and stopped talking in the middle of her sentence. "Ah . . . hum . . . yes, Jones. At ease, please."

In a system as rigidly structured as the navy, the unexpected always creates tension. No one had ever interrupted the "morality lecture" with a question. No one had ever asked a question. It was the navy's duty to warn the recruits that the very behavior the navy condoned, even encouraged them to pursue with sailors, was a criminal offense with other women. It was their duty to warn in as oblique a manner as possible, and the recruits' duty to listen. No one ever mentioned the word *lesbian*. But the message was that if you were one, don't get caught. And if you weren't a lesbian, watch out because they'll get you. The tension in the room was palpable.

Jones smiled her most winning smile. "I just wanted to make sure that I was following you, ma'am."

The officer nodded for Jones to continue.

"Now, you're saying that in the navy, if a woman hugs another woman, or kisses her, or maybe even says she loves her, the navy is going to call that woman a lesbian. And that being a lesbian is a criminal offense, and the navy will kick you out, or put you in jail?"

The officer hesitated before replying. "That is certainly the risk."

"So, that if I stand here and tell you that I love my friend, Harper," Jones dropped her hand to Harper's shoulder, who sat just in front of her, "you're going to take me to jail?" She held her hands before her as if handcuffed already. "Well, you better take me, cause I've loved Harper since we were ten years old."

The officer shook her head and started to reply.

"And if the navy wants to label that unnatural, they won't be the first, and it won't stop me loving her." Jones placed one hand on her hip. "My own mama said to me when I first brought Harper home, 'Now, honey, why do you insist on hanging around with that poor white girl. It just seems unnatural the way you two carry on.' But I didn't listen to her eight years ago because I knew how I felt was one of the most natural things I'd ever known. Eight years later, Mama says I am lucky to have a friend like Harper. And I am. But if I'd listened to her, where would I be now? So, I ask you, in the most sincere way possible, you think I'll let the navy tell me who to be friends with, or how to go about it?" Jones sat down slowly, as if to emphasize her point.

Weston was grinning from ear to ear. She was jubilant. She felt they should all leap to their feet and give Jones a standing, thunderous ovation. It was time someone publicly drew the line. It was fine for the navy to concoct rules and regulations governing uniforms, military decorum, and the assorted diddly things that kept admirals happy. For her, the time had come to begin to redefine her contract with the navy. It employed her only; it did not own her. This was what the torment of the last few weeks had been about. She suddenly recognized that kissing Harper had irrevocably shifted her perceptions, her expectations of the world, and, most importantly, of herself. She could not change what she had discovered of herself these last few weeks. Given the opportunity, she was not sure she would want to. Instead, she would change the world, start a revolution in the great American tradition. And Jones had just fired the first shot.

As she looked around her, Weston saw only fear and anger on most of the faces of her fellow recruits. There was surprise on Yont's. Taylor had her head in her hand, so her reaction was unreadable. Bates was laughing, it seemed in delight, and Kiel appeared furious. None seemed to mirror Weston's enthusiasm. The tension had grown unbearable.

The good-looking officer no longer lounged against the edge of the desk. She stood ramrod straight by its side, the fingertips of her left hand just grazing the surface of the desk top, as if grounding herself. "Well, of course the navy isn't saying that ladies in the services cannot be friends, recruit Jones. It always encourages its recruits to make and keep girlfriends in the forces, as actively as . . . ," here she struggled a bit for the exact phrase that would perfectly summarize the navy's position, "as actively as it discourages other types of relationships."

Weston inspected the faces of the other recruits in the room as the officer finished her speech. Am I the only one, she wondered, who has begun to question what business it is of the military's in the first place?

27

★ ★ ☆

"Shit, that dagger's got some nerve, hey?" Taylor giggled.

"Oh, Jones is no dagger," Weston stated emphatically.

Taylor eyed her carefully through the cloud of cigarette smoke that layered the air between them. "Oh?" she added archly. "And who elected you the resident authority?" There was a long pause while Weston's face colored brightly. Taylor winked broadly and patted her hand. "So, you done learned more than how to march at bootcamp, huh sailor?" She shook her head, "Phew, beats me where you found the time. But I say, good on you darlin." She smiled at Weston's discomfort with genuine affection.

"Jeez, Taylor, give me a break." Weston finally broke the silence. "I was just so proud of Jones. Weren't you? I thought the whole room would jump to its feet and give her a standing ovation." Weston's eyes were bright with recalled excitement.

Taylor laughed outright. "Some things never change." She chuckled, "Only you could come up with such a notion." She reached for the package of cigarettes and pulled another from the pack. Her eyes sparkled as she lit her smoke. "Did you catch Kiel's expression after that class?"

"Boy, I've never seen her so mad."

"Mad? She was furious." Taylor exhaled. "This past week has been a bit of a trial for her, but that class was the last straw. She would have marched us all off the edge of a very high cliff if she could have found one handy."

Taylor shook her head and sighed. "Course, ole Jones has cooked her own goose as far as the navy's concerned. If they hadn't given those two separate duty stations before, they'll never leave them together now."

Weston grew thoughtful and leaned her head back against the wall. "I wonder if Jones had thought of that before her little tirade." Silence greeted her question, so she continued. "I guess that's how they keep us quiet. The implication is that if we rock the boat, the consequences will be so stupendously awful that our present misery would look good by comparison. Don't you think?" She turned and looked at Taylor with raised eyebrows.

Taylor's face wore a quizzical expression. "Where have you *been* the last two weeks?" She hugged Weston's shoulder and moaned mockingly, "My baby's growing up right before my very eyes."

Weston shoved her away. "Go away. It's obvious that you're not into deep philosophical ramblings tonight." She laughed and handed Taylor one of her own cigarettes. "Here, have one. I have a little story that I want to tell you."

Taylor raised an eyebrow but lit the cigarette and settled back against the washroom wall.

Weston took a deep breath. "You know I grew up in Arizona." Taylor nodded. "And that my dad could never hang onto a job, so we were always moving from town to town. Mostly we ended up on the wrong side of the tracks where the rents are really cheap. 'Mexicantown,' most towns had one." Weston leaned back against the wall. "I never thought much about it as a kid."

Weston ran her fingers through her hair and continued. "I

must have been about twelve and we had lived in one place for nearly three years and I finally had real friends. Lupe, Maria, and Jesus were all kids from my neighborhood."

Taylor exhaled loudly, "Yeah, so?"

Weston rolled her eyes at Taylor in reply. "Anyway, this was around the time that color TVs started to come on the market. Hardly anyone could afford them at first, remember? Ours was mostly a rural town with farmers and ranchers making all the money. People like us who lived in town were mostly seasonal workers or dimestore employees. My mom was a secretary.

"One day, one of my schoolmates, a rancher's daughter, decided to throw a party because they did, indeed, get a color TV. First one on the block, you know? Actually, the first one in the valley. And they wanted everyone to know. So, one day after school she's standing by the door handing out invitations. I was just getting ready to leave and I could feel her looking at me. Deciding. Then she comes over and slaps one on my desk and leaves."

Taylor noncommittally said, "Uh-huh."

"I didn't open it right away. Didn't know what it was. Once I did though, I was really excited. It said to come over on Sunday night to watch 'Bonanza' in color. Her mom would make popcorn. God, I was excited. 'Bonanza' was my very favorite. I couldn't wait for Sunday.

"Of course, when I got home and told my mom she didn't quite believe it. She called up the girl's mother. She said, oh yes *everyone* in the class was invited. It would be a nice outing for them all. And no, she didn't think it was too much trouble. When Sunday came my mom starched and ironed a clean blouse for me and made me wear new jeans. She was certainly more nervous than I was when she dropped me off at the rancher's big house."

Weston paused. She could hear Taylor lighting a new cigarette.

"*Well,* what happened?"

"Huh. Oh, well. I got there just as 'Bonanza' was starting. You know how the map of Virginia City catches on fire in the middle and burns all up? I remember thinking, wow, it looks just like real fire. And then, in the middle come all the Cartwrights. And I finally got to see what color Little Joe's horse was, that he was always running everywhere. Part of me always felt a little sorry for that horse. And I laughed at all the funny bits and never thought anything about it. Except that it was just like being at the Cartwrights' ranch, seeing it all in color.

"The lights came on when it was over, and they passed popcorn around. Then it hit me. I didn't know a single kid there. I mean, I knew them because we were in the same classroom at school. But there was no one from around where I lived. And all of a sudden I knew exactly what that little rich girl had been thinking before she handed me the invitation. She was weighing if I counted or not, and I passed because I was white."

Silence. "Just what are you trying to say, Weston?" Taylor eyed her companion speculatively.

"I'm not really sure myself." Weston paused and thought. "I think for years I've known the difference between myself and those childhood friends. You can't grow up in Arizona and not know—"

"So. What's the good in knowing?" Taylor interrupted harshly.

The faucet at the far end of the washroom dripped methodically, accenting the quiet. Weston appraised Taylor with solemn eyes. "I suppose there's no good at all in knowing," she scratched her temple slowly, "if it only gets buried again. If it's covered over with mindless excuses." She exhaled dramatically. "I guess that's what I'm trying to say. That. . . I'll try not to let that happen ever again."

Taylor stubbed out her cigarette in the basin and reached for Weston's hand. She squinted one eye and tightened her grip, "Well, that's something, anyway. A damn sight more than anyone else has ever promised." They sat in companionable silence. Taylor lit another cigarette. "So, you ready to do some dirt?"

"Dirt?" Weston queried.

Taylor laughed. "Yeah, did you hear the latest adventure of our company's master fornicator?"

"Bates?"

"Who else?"

They talked. The talked to catch up on all the important stuff that no one else had seen or thought significant to comment about. They talked about the fleet and where their careers would take them. Already there was talk about life after the navy. Speculation was their favorite game, and they both played it with an intensity and enthusiasm that they seldom encountered outside themselves. And sometimes they just sat in silence for long moments and enjoyed sharing the quiet that pushes the night gently toward dawn.

A watchstander poked her head into the washroom. "Reveille in ten minutes, ladies."

Taylor and Weston looked at each other and laughed. They slid off the counter together and clasped arms and danced around the washroom. "We made it. We made it." They sang, delirious. Dizzy and out of breath they leaned once more against the counter. "I guess I better go and wake up the troops or they'll never forgive me," Weston sighed. She quickly grabbed Taylor and hugged her. "Thanks, forever." And kissed her on the cheek.

Taylor slapped Weston on the bum. "Go on. Get out of here."

28

★ ★ ☆

Weston sat on the edge of her suitcase in the airport terminal, waiting for her flight to be called. Her hat brim was squared straight across her eyebrows. Her oxfords gleamed in the cold, fluorescent light, and one immaculate white glove was draped across her knee as she puffed on her last cigarette. A parting gift from Taylor.

Of course, she had been right. When they received their orders just prior to the graduation ceremony, Harper and Jones discovered they had been stationed at opposite ends of the country. The navy's buddy system for women recruits was only honored for the duration of bootcamp. After that, they could do with you what they wanted.

Taylor had graduated top of her class. Weston smiled to herself at the thought. In spite of her anger, her frustration, her disappointment, Taylor was still able to push herself to excel. What incredible will and strength of character that took. That woman wouldn't clerk at Macy's; she would own it. Bates was going to radioman's school, which meant she would stay on at Bainbridge. She had seemed genuinely pleased with her orders. Yont had requested a southern duty station and gotten it. And herself? Weston exhaled a puff of smoke. She was going to Florida. Photo school. Warm weather and beaches. She had graduated in the top ten percent and had received an extra stripe for her efforts. Langhard had acted like it was a big deal.

Taylor had scoffed as they had sown the stripes on their uniforms before graduation. "Just give me the money. Course it means we won't have to make the coffee quite as often, neither."

The ceremony itself had been a lark. It wasn't supposed to be. It was grave and somber with lots of visiting officers and parents, of course. Speeches that went on forever while the recruits stood in full uniform, the whole duration of the two-and-a-half-hour ceremony, in the drillhall that now sweltered in the heat of an instantaneous spring.

The drill team had accidentally provided them with a moment of almost unbearable humor. These young women practiced for hours each day honing their responses to an intricate set of commands to peak perfection for display each graduation day. Every recruit knew the routine from hours of repetition, but a very select group performed for the dignitaries. It was supposed to be a flawless display of military precision.

She and Taylor had decided that it was almost too appropriate that on this day there was the tiniest error—with major consequences. Every recruit knew the commands, could do them in her sleep because the sequence was always the same. You *never* had to guess what was coming next. You merely had to wait for the order to give you the timing to execute the maneuver. The first half of the exhibition had gone quite well, the recruits acting as well-oiled automatons. Just as the drill team marched directly in front of the raised dais where the most important guests sat, the drill team commander shouted the order for a tricky bit of footwork. It was out of order and was appropriately named mass confusion.

Each recruit, within the unit, was supposed to execute an individual action that took them to the four corners of the drillhall and inexplicably led them back into a cohesive unit. It was wonderful. No one knew what to do. Some recruits balked at doing anything and just stood there. Some tried to execute the order given. Others were determined to perform the movement that should have been called.

Taylor and Weston were in near hysteria as they watched the frantic efforts of the other recruits. Their timing, the pacing, was so ingrained from the hours of repetition that they managed to reassemble and continue without a hitch to the next correct call. The dignitaries applauded appreciatively. Half the senior class wept with laughter; the other half wept with fury at their despoiled graduation.

And then, it was all over. Weston and Taylor had hugged shyly, neither knowing what to say at the end, when they had spent so many hours talking. Jones was direct, to the point. Harper had held her shoulders with firm hands on saying good-bye, and it had both embarrassed Weston and excited her. The feeling was bittersweet. Harper was being sent as far west as the navy could manage without bestowing an overseas assignment. They all guessed that they would never meet again and that in itself made farewells more difficult. To have shared so much and yet, in the end, it was made to seem like nothing at all.

Weston sighed and stubbed out her cigarette. She was truly, literally, alone. She felt like a mother hen must whose chicks have hatched and been taken elsewhere. She almost missed the constant clucking and pecking about her skirts. Almost. But certainly not enough to start another brood anytime soon.

"Cigarette?" The voice was hopeful, wistful.

Weston raised her eyes past the thirteen navy-blue buttons on blue wool pants. Careful blue eyes appraised her. Weston scanned the airport waiting room. She was the only woman for miles.

She met the young sailor's gaze and without apology or reproach said, "I don't smoke."